ORIENT EXPRESS

ORIENT EXPRESS

A TRAVEL MEMOIR

John Dos Passos

Copyright © 1922, 1927 by John Dos Passos

Cover illustration by John Dos Passos

Cover design by Kat JK Lee

ISBN: 978-1-5040-1148-8

Distributed in 2015 by Open Road Distribution
345 Hudson Street
New York, NY 10014
www.openroadmedia.com

CONTENTS

ORIENT EXPRESS

I. EASTWARD

1. PICO

Hoity-toity
Cha de noite
Sea's still high
An' sky's all doity

they sang as they propped themselves against the bar and fought seasickness with madeira. On the bench opposite the other passengers sat in a row with green faces. Every long roll of the Mormugaõ ended in a lurch and a nasty rattling of busted clockwork from the direction of the engineroom. Outside, the wind yelled and the spray flew as the boat wallowed deeper and deeper in the trough of the sea; inside, the madeira got lower and lower in the dark amber bottle and the eastbound Americans sang louder and louder into the twitching pea-green faces of the other passengers propped in a row

Sea's still high
An' sky's all doity.

Later we are driving along over a huge easy gradual swell with a moist west wind behind us. The madeira is all drunk up. Sky and

3

sea are blurred in a great sweeping scud, silver as thistledown in the hidden moonlight. In that scud the shoving wetnosed wind is carrying spring eastward to fall in rain on Lisbon, San Vicente, Madrid, to beat against windows in Marseilles and Rome, to quicken the thrusting sprouts in weedy cemeteries in Stamboul. Now and then the scud breaks and a tiny round moon shows through among whorls and spirals of speeding mist that thickens into sagging clots and thins into long spaces bright and crinkly as tinfoil.

The bow quivers as it nuzzles deep into each new lunging hill. A squall hides the moon and spatters my head nervously with rain and rushes on leaving some streaks of clear moonlight eastward where the islands are. Then we are driving along muffled in thistledown mist again. I have fallen asleep huddled in the V of the bow.

When I open my eyes the wind has stopped. Only a few patches of scud swirl eastward overhead. The huge swells are bright and heavy like mercury in the still moonlight. It isn't a sound coming across the water, it's a smell, a growing fragrance beating against my face on a burst of warm air out of the east, a smell of roses and dung burnt by the sun, a rankness like skunk-cabbage overlaid with hyacinth, pungence of musk, chilly sweetness of violets. Hours later, eastward we made out, wrapped in clouds, the dark cone of Pico.

2. TERMINUS MARITIME

At Ostend the boat for the Continent lands alongside of a tall black hotel. After they have gone through the customs and had their passports stamped the passengers for Central Europe and the Orient file through the tall tragic black doorway into a vast restaurant thinly sprinkled with round tables. They sit at the tables and a sound of talk in various languages drifts up into the high coffered ceiling and out over the dark squares of the rainlashed harbor. People order food and eat it hurriedly with an occasional nervous glance at the clock. Having eaten they take their places, which they have previously reserved with pieces of baggage, in the various trains. The trains are rather empty, all the lean windows of the hotel are closed with dark grey shutters, the great squares of the harbor are empty. A conductor with gold braid on his cap paces back and forth on the platform, occasionally stroking the bristles of a rusty moustache.

At the other end of the platform beside a slot machine is a large thermometer constructed, so it announces in red letters, by Monsieur Guépratte, that gives you the chilliness in Centigrade, Fahrenheit, and Réaumur degrees and adds little informatory mottoes such as that 60° is the mean temperature of Pondichéry, that 35° is best for an ordinary bath, that silkworms are happiest at 25°, and also sickrooms.

It is not traintime yet. The eastbound American goes back through the portals of doom into the empty restaurant where in the arctic stillness a lone waiter stands beside a table teetering like a penguin. He sits down beside the waiter and orders a brandy and soda, telling himself with passionate melancholy that 60° is the mean temperature of Pondichéry. If it's sixty in the shade in Pondichéry how cold does it have to be to freeze vodka in Nijni Novgorod? Answer me that Michel Strogoff.

Through the doorway I can read the bronze letters on the wet side of the sleeping car, *Compagnie Internationale des Wagons Lits et des Grands Expresses Européens.* A gust of wet air slaps me in the face from time to time, bringing a smell of varnish and axlegrease and couplings, a smell of departure and distance that evokes a very small boy being coaxed trembling onto a new huge shining train in a shed somewhere. A train fresh painted fresh varnished that smells like new rubber balls, like tin toys, like sewing machines, a train that is going to start but that never starts. We're going to move. The engine whistles long. We're off. No it's only the walls moving, towns and mountains and trees and rivers moving: Panorama of the Trans-Siberian.

En voiture messieurs, mesdames. . . . The eastbound American is yanked to his feet, spills money for his drink onto the table, runs out through the tall portal down the wet platform, boards the train that has begun very slowly to move.

3. LUNA

Dinner alone beside a pink and yellow lampshade (categoria de lusso), out of the window the colored postcard of San Giorgio Maggiore. Venice the Coney Island of Coney Islands, the Midway of history built for goggle-eyed westerners out of the gaudy claptrap of the east, and through it all the smell of tidewater, rotting piles, mudflats, a gruff bodysmell under the lipstick and perfume and ricepowder, a smell desolately amorous like chestnut blooms, like datura, like trodden cabbages. Women passing on the quai wear their hair fluffed up the way the prostitutes in Carpaccio's pictures do, and long black silk shawls with fringes longer than the fringes of the shawls of the women of Seville; their skin is a firm yellowish color and they have straight ivory noses. An occasional flicker of lightning behind the dome and tapering tower of San Giorgio reveals the fact that it is merely a cutout, that the water is an excellently contrived effect, that the people on the quai are an opera chorus intermingled with a few supers, that the moon is a baby spot.

I hustle out of the restaurant for fear the act will be over, walk hastily along overhung streets, over humped bridges, down alleys where through tavern doorways you can see people drinking at long varnished tables. Red-haired girls behind bars, drunken men playing guitars in front of a cathouse by the waterside, clanging smells of wine and garlic; in every direction spaghetti-tenors singing in boats. In the piazza an orchestra playing William Tell for all it's worth, on the Grand Canal Santa Lucia carried high by a soprano above a croaking of fat basses. In the sky the electrician has killed the moon. I can make out the big and the little Dipper in a spangled black cyclorama. In the canals the ripple of water would be as excellently imitated as in the Nile scene from "Aida," if it weren't for the inexorable smell of the tide creeping up slimecovered steps, of mudflats and waterlogged barges, chilly hands of the Adriatic groping for your throat.

Florian's; broad shirtfronts of waiters, icecream-colored parasols, women in fluffy summer clothes, white flannels, under a grey sky that someone at the top of the Campanile has suddenly filled with fluttering green, pink, yellow papers that ultimately light among the tables announcing Lulli's toilet articles. Young men swagger in fours and fives through the crowds singing Giovanezza, giovanezza. Somewhere behind the ornate facades, in alleys hidden away so as not to scare the tourists, there is fighting going on. There is something in the air that makes you uncomfortable in the aviary twitter of Florian's. On every bare wall there are signs VV LENIN or M LENIN. I wander irresolutely about over the marble pavements through the dying light of a yellow sunset. A boat with an ochre sail that has a great crimson patch in the middle of it proceeds slowly across the daffodil water, a black barge with four men rowing in effortless unison crawls away towards the Lido. Under an archway behind me some people are looking at a pasquinade scrawled in black chalk. The words are in English in thick rounded letters:

THIS BUNDLE MUST DIE

Aha, says the stiffwhiskered gentleman in a straw hat addressing the crowd, That means in English, Death to the Socialisti.

4. Express

Joggling three times a day in a dining car. First through the Kingdom of the Serbs, Croats and Slovenes, then through Bulgaria and a slice of Greece. There's the lady from Wellesley who writes for the Atlantic Monthly; an egg-shaped Armenian from New York who was brought up at the monastery of San Lazzaro in Venice, studied painting in Asolo, hates priests, clergymen and Balkan cookery and talks plaintively of Tiffany's and old Martin's restaurant on 28th Street; there's another Armenian whose mother, father and three sisters were cut up into little pieces before his eyes by the Turks in Trebizond; there's a tall iron-grey Standard Oil man, very tall with a little pot belly the shape of half a football. He says he can size up people at a glance and he sits all day writing doggerel descriptive of his travels to his favorite niece. Then there's a man with many seals on his watch who looks like a 14th Street auctioneer, and two scrawny colonial Englishwomen; all these against a changing background of sallow Balkan people with big noses and dark rings under their eyes.

Between meals I sit in the privacy of my little green compartment full of nickel knobs and fixings reading Diehl, who is very dull, occasionally interrupted by passport men, customs agents, detectives, secret police or by the porter, an elderly Belgian who breathes heavily like a locomotive, a man irrevocably exhausted by too many miles of railroad, by too many telegraph poles counted, by too many cinders brushed off green plush seats. At stations I walk up and down with a brittle Frenchman smoking the local cigarettes; he talks knowingly about Bucharest, love, assassination, triangular marriage and diplomacy. He knows everything and his collars and cuffs are always spotless. His great phrase is Aller dans le luxe . . . Il faut toujours aller dans le luxe.

Day by day the hills get scrawnier and dryer and the train goes more and more slowly and the stationmasters have longer and longer moustaches and seedier and seedier uniforms until at last we are winding between a bright-green sea and yellow sunburned capes. Suddenly the train is trapped between mustard-colored crumbling walls, the line runs among rubbish heaps and cypresses. The train is hardly moving at all, it stops imperceptibly as if on a siding. Is it? No, yes, it must be . . . Constantinople.

II. CONSTANT' JULY 1921

1. PERA PALACE

Under my window a dusty rutted road with here and there a solitary pavingstone over which carts jolt and jingle continually, climbing jerkily to Pera, rumbling down towards the old bridge, all day long from dawn to dusk; beyond, tall houses closer-packed than New York houses even, a flat roof where a barelegged girl hangs out laundry, and across red tiles the dusty cypresses of a cemetery, masts, and the Golden Horn, steel-colored, with steamers at anchor; and, further, against the cloudy sky, Stamboul, domes, brown-black houses, bright minarets set about everywhere like the little ivory men on a cribbage board. Up the road where it curves round the cemetery of the Petits Champs—more dusty cypresses, stone posts with turbans carved on them tilting this way and that—carts are dumping rubbish down the hill, ashes, rags, papers, things that glitter in the sunlight; as fast as they are dumped women with sacks on their backs, scrambling and elbowing each other, pick among the refuse with lean hands. A faint rasping of querulous voices drifts up from them amid the cries of vegetable-sellers and the indeterminate swarming rumor of many lives packed into narrow streets.

Thum-rum-tum: thum-rum-tum on an enormous tambourine and the conquering whine of a bagpipe. Two tall men with gaudy turbans round their fezzes come out of a lane leading a monkey. The thumping, wheezing tune is the very soul of the monkey's listless irregular walk. Carters stop their carts. Beggars jump up from where they had been crouching by the shady wall. The ragpickers try to straighten their bent backs and shade their eyes against the sun to see. Waiters in dress-suits hang out from the windows of the hotel. Taking advantage of the crowd, two men carrying a phonograph with a white enamelled horn on a sort of a table with handles, set it down and start it playing an amazing tune like a leaky water-faucet. The tall men with the monkey thump their tambourine in derision and swagger away.

Downstairs in the red plush lobby of the Pera Palace there is scuttling and confusion. They are carrying out a man in a frock coat who wears on his head a black astrakhan cap. There's blood in the red plush armchair; there's blood on the mosaic floor. The manager walks back and forth with sweat standing out on his brow; they can mop up the floor but the chair is ruined. French, Greek and Italian gendarmes swagger about talking all together each in his own language. The poor bloke's dead, sir, says the British M.P. to the colonel who doesn't know whether to finish his cocktail or not. Azerbaidjan. Azerbaidjan. He was the envoy from Azerbaidjan. An Armenian, a man with a beard, stood in the doorway and shot him. A man with glasses and a smooth chin, a Bolshevik spy, walked right up to him and shot him. The waiter who brings drinks from the bar is in despair. The drinkers have all left without paying.

2. Jardin de Taxim

A table under a striped umbrella at the edge of the terrace of the restaurant at Taxim Garden (Entrée 5 piastres, libre aux militaires). Dardenella from a Russian orchestra. On the slope below a fence made of hammered-out Standard Oil tins encloses a mud hut beside which a donkey grazes. Two men squat placidly on the slope at the gate and look out, across some tacky little villas, like villas at Nice, and a gas tank streaked red with fresh paint, at the Bosphorus and the Asian hills. It is nearly dark. The Bosphorus shines about the string of grey battleships at anchor. Between the brown hills in the foreground and the blue hills in the distance curls up a thick pillar of smoke. One thinks of villages burning, but this is too far to the north, and they have a habit at this season in the back country of burning off the hills to smoke out brigands. The orchestra is resting for a moment. From the yellow barracks to the left comes a tune on a hurdygurdy and a quavering voice singing.

Then the rim of an enormous bloodorange moon rolls up out of Asia.

Presently when one has eaten caviar and pilaf and sword-fish from the Black Sea washed down by Nectar beer, made at the edge of town in the brewery of a certain gentleman of immeasurable wealth named Bomonti, the show begins on the stage among the trees. International vaudeville. First a Russian lady waves a green hand-kerchief in a peasant dance with a certain timid grace one feels sure was learned at some fashionable dancing academy in Moscow. Then two extraordinarily tough English girls in socks and jumpers, per-haps ex of the pony ballet at the Folies Bergères. One of them croons in a curious bored and jerky manner as they go through the steps and kicking that shocked country parsons at the Gaiety when Queen Victoria was a girl. Then come Greek acrobats, a comic Russian lady understood only by her compatriots, a Frenchwoman in black with operatic arms and a conservatoire manner who sings the mad scene from "Lucia" several times to huge applause, a pitiful little woman in pink tulle dancing the Moment Musicale with that peculiar inanity of gesture encouraged by dancing instructresses in American state capitals, and so on endlessly.

Meanwhile people move about the gardens among the locusttrees; jokes are passed, drinks poured. There are flirtations, pairings off. Three girls arm in arm dart into a side path followed by three Italian sailors, brown sinewy youngsters in white suits. A party of Greek offi-cers are very gay. Their army has taken Eski Chehir. The Kemalists are about to leave Ismid. Tino is a great king after all. Opposite them two elderly Turkish gentlemen in frock coats and white vests pull impas-sively on their narghiles. Further back seven gobs are getting noisily drunk at a round table. Toward the gate stands an Italian gendarme, imported all complete from the buttons on his coattails to his shiny tricorne, and a British M.P. with A.P.C. (standing for Allied Police Commission) in handsome letters on his sleeve.

Why do you want to learn Turkish? a Greek girl asks me, a look of puzzled irritation on her face. You must side with the Greeks; you mustn't learn Turkish.

Flits through my head a memory of the little yellow tables and chairs under the great planetree beside the mosque of Bayazid over in Stamboul, the pigeons, and the old men with beards as white as their white cotton turbans who sat there gravely nodding their heads in endless slow discussions; and how a beggar inconceivably old, yellow like frayed damask, gnarled like a dying plumtree, had asked for a light from my cigarette and then smiling had pointed to the glass of water that stood beside my little coffeecup, and how when I had handed him the water, he had had to crouch low to the ground to drink it, his back was so bent; and the gesture full of sceptered kings with which he had put back the glass and thanked me with a wave of a skinny corded hand. There was something in that wave of the hand of the soaring of minarets and the cry of muezzins and the impassive eyes of the elderly Turkish gentlemen in white vests sitting so quiet beside rejoicing Greeks in the Jardin de Taxim. There are reasons for learning Turkish.

Then when one has seen all one can stand of international vaudeville, of Russian ladies trying to earn a few pennies for the hard bread of exile, of Levantine dancers and beached European singers, one walks home along the Grande Rue de Pera. Along the curbs are more Russian refugees, soldiers in varied worn uniforms that once were Wrangel's army, selling everything imaginable out of little trays slung about their necks—paper flowers and kewpie dolls, shoelaces and jumping jacks and little colored silhouettes under glass of mosques and cypresses, and cakes round and square and lifepreserver-shaped. They are men of all ages and conditions, mostly with dense white northern skins and fair close-cropped hair, all with a drawn hungry look about the cheekbones and a veiled shudder of pain in their eyes. In the restaurants one can see through the open windows pale girls with veils bound tight about their hair. On the arms of two stout Armenians two rouged and densely powdered ladies in twin dresses of flounced pink ride out of an alleyway on the jingling waves that spurt from a mechanical piano.

Further along a onelegged Russian soldier stands against a lamppost, big red hands covering his face, and sobs out loud.

3. MASSACRE

The red plush salon of the Pera Palace Hotel. The archbishop, a tall man in flowing black with a beautiful curly chestnut-colored beard and gimlet eyes, is pouring out an impetuous torrent of Greek. Listening to him a Greek lady elaborately dressed in rose satin, an American naval officer, a journalist, some miscellaneous frockcoated people. Clink of ice in highballs being brought to two British majors across the room. The archbishop lifts a slender Byzantine hand and orders coffee. Then he changes to French, lisping a little his long balanced phrases, in which predominate the words *horreur, atrocité, œuvre humanitaire, civilisation mondiale.* The Turks in Samsoun, the Kemalists, who some weeks since deported the men of orthodox faith, have now posted an order to deport the women and children. Three days' notice. Of course that means . . . Massacre, says someone hastily.

The archbishop's full lips are at the rim of his tiny coffeecup. He drinks quickly and meticulously. In one's mind beyond the red plush a vision of dark crowds crawling inland over sunshrivelled hills. The women were crying and wailing in the streets of Samsoun, says the officer. The news must be sent out, continues the archbishop; the world must know the barbarity of the Turks; America must know. A telegram to the President of the United States must be sent off. Again in one's mind beyond red plush salons, and the polished phrases of official telegrams, the roads at night under the terrible bloodorange moon of Asia, and the wind of the defiles blowing dust among huddled women, stinging the dark attentive eyes of children, and far off on the heatbaked hills a sound of horsemen.

In a big armchair beside the window a Turk with grizzled eyebrows and with eyes as soft and as brown as the archbishop's beard looks

JOHN DOS PASSOS

unmovedly at nothing. One by one the oval amber beads of a conversation chaplet drop through his inscrutably slow white fingers.

4. ASSASSINATION

Extracts from a letter published under "Tribune Libre" in the *Presse du Soir* that comes out in Pera every evening with two pages of French and four of Russian:

The eighteenth of June my husband, Bekhboud Djevanchir Khan, was murdered.

I the undersigned, his wife, of Russian origin, trust to your kindness for the publication of certain facts which will put an end I hope to the false rumors that are attainting the dead man's good name.

I have never been separated from my husband and God has made me witness of all the horror of these last years.

March 1918. The wreck of the Russian army crawling back from the Turkish front. At Baku the power is in the hands of Armenians who have adopted the Bolshevist platform. By order of no one knows who, according to a prearranged plan, there is organized a massacre of the Muslim population.

Never till my last breath shall I forget those terrible days. They were tracking my husband; his name was on the list of the proscribed. By a miracle he escaped. We fled the town and after unbelievable privations, succeeded in getting to Elisabethpol.

Months passed. Power changed hands, and my husband was called to the post of Minister of the Interior in the first Azerbaidjan cabinet. Turkish detachments draw near to Baku and again, before they reach the town, the bloody happenings of September are unrolled. It was the terrible reply of the Muslims to the March massacres.

My husband hastens to Baku to put an end to these riots, but by the time he arrives the wave of national hatred has subsided. National hate gives way to class hate; the Bolsheviki aspire towards power and the local population, tired of national and religious strife, see in the Reds a neutral force.

In the beginning of 1920, the Bolsheviki have control and start settling their scores with the representatives of the national parties. We are driven out of our house; everything we have is taken from us. My husband is arrested by the extraordinary commission and sentenced to death. But the particular conditions in Baku and his great influence oblige the Soviet powers to free him. In spite of his reiterated solicitations they refuse to let him leave the country, knowing that he is a mining engineer and one of the best specialists on the naphtha industry. Fate itself reserves for him the rôle of "spec." He is offered a post in the commissariat of foreign affairs which offers possibilities of a foreign mission.

My husband accepts and some time afterwards we leave for Constantinople. Here death awaited him: an assassin's hand ended the life of my husband whose only crime was to love above all things his people and his country, to which he had consecrated his studies, his work and all his life.

Two words more on the subject of the rumors that my husband had betrayed his companions of the "Moussavat" party, and that for this they had condemned him to death. In the eyes of those who have even slightly known the defunct, these rumors are so absurd that they are not worth the trouble of denying. Such gossip will not be able to tarnish, in the hearts of those who intimately knew him, the glorious memory of the defunct.

I am, yours etc.

5. THE CRESCENT

They sell amber beads and the notaries and scribes have their little tables and stools in the court of the mosque of Bayazid. Charitable people have left foundations for the feeding of the pigeons that circle among the dappled branches of its planes and perch, drinking, beaks tilted up, throats shimmering with each swallow, on the marble verge of its washing fountain. One flaring noon I stood against the cold granite of a column watching a Bedoueen in a stiff bournous of white wool dictate a letter to a scribe with the gestures of an emperor composing an edict to a conquered city, when I noticed that a constant string of people was going in under the high portal of the mosque. Adventuring inquisitively near, I was beckoned in by a young man who dangled a green silk tassel at the end of his string of amber beads. An old man obsequiously pushed big slippers over my shoes, and I stepped over the high threshold. The huge red-carpeted floor under the dome and the dais along the sides were full of men, beggars and porters and artisans in leather aprons and small boys with fezzes too large for their bullet heads and stately gentlemen in frock coats and white vests with festooned watch chains and gravebearded theological students in neatly wound white cotton turbans, all squatting close together with their shoes beside them. A yellowbright beam of sunlight striking across the pearly shimmer of the dome gave full on the bronze face and shining beard of the mollah who was reading the Koran and brought fierce magenta flame into the silk hanging that fell from the front of the pulpit platform. He read in a wooden staccato voice, swaying slightly with the rhythm, and in the pause at the end of each verse a soft Ameen growled through the crowd.

—It is for the fall of Adrianople, this day every year, the young man with the green tassel on his beads whispered in French in my ear—Many of these people come from Adrianople, fled from the Greeks. . . . Commemoration.

The man who had been reading climbed down clumsily across the magenta silk hanging and a taller man with full lips and dark cheeks flushed under hollow eyes took his place.

—Now he will pray for the army in Anatolia.

His body erect, his eyes staring straight into the sunlight, his hands raised level with his beard in the attitude of prayer, the new mollah shouted a prayer full of harsh ringing consonants and brazen upward cadences. His voice was like warhorns and kettledrums. And all through the mosque under the faintly blue dome men looked beyond the palms of their raised hands at the flaming magenta silk and the priest praying in the yellow shaft of sunlight, and the Ameen at every pause rose from a growl to a roar, grew fierce and breathless till the little glass lamps tinkled in the huge flat chandeliers above the turbans and the fezzes, rolled up the stucco walls, shook the great dome as the domes of the churches must have shaken with the shout of the fighting-men of Islam the day Constantine's city was carried by assault and the last Constantine killed in his purple boots.

At the door as they left everyone was presented with a card on which was a cut of the great mosque of Adrianople, and with a small tissuepaper bag of candies.

6. DOUZICO

A fragile savor comes from the tiny rounded leaves of the basil in a pot on the edge of the café table. Behind on a little platform fenced with red baize, musicians keep up a reiterant humming and twanging out of which a theme in minor climbs and skids in an endless arabesque. There is a kind of lute, a zither, a violin and a woman who sings. In the midst is a stool with coffeecups and a bottle of mastic. The zither is played by a grizzled man with a bottlenose and spectacles who occasionally throws his head back and opens his mouth wide and lets out happily a great Gregorian yodel which the other voices follow and lead back with difficulty into the web of sound. At the tables packed under the locusttree where they will get shade in the afternoon sit people with narghiles or cigarettes or German pipes or American cigars drinking mastic and beer and coffee and even vodka. There is a smell of tobacco and charcoal and anis from the mastic and douzico and grilled meat from the skewers of chiche kebab, and a discordance of many hostile languages and a shuffle of feet from the street under the terrace.

Leaning my chin on my hands and looking down at the strip of cracked and dusty pavement between the bare feet of the boys who sell cakes and pistachio nuts and flyspotted candy along the terrace wall, and the row of autos for hire, of which the drivers, mostly Russians in various patched uniforms, loll and sleep and chat, waiting for a fare through the long afternoon hours. . . . Across that space shoes, feet, shambling legs, crossed arms, arms swinging vacantly, stoop shoulders, strongly moulded backs under thin cotton, chests brown, sweatbeaded, shawls, black veils of women, yakmaks, faces. All life is sucked into the expressiveness of faces. A boy, skin the color of an earthen pot,

17

eyes and lips of a drunken Bacchus, swaggers by jauntily, on his head a tray of roasted yellow corn. A girl patters along, mouse-like, features droop white as a freesia behind a thin black veil. A whitebearded man in a blue gown, redrimmed eyes as bleared as moonstones, being led by a tiny brown boy. Two hammals, each strong enough to carry a piano alone, with deeplymarked mindless features, and the black beards of Assyrian bowmen. Three Russians, blond, thick-chested of the same height, white canvas tunics pulled down tight under their belts, blue eyes, with a freshwashed look and their hair parted and slicked like children dressed for a party. A stout Greek businessman in a Palm Beach suit. Tommies very pink and stiff. Aggressive thickjawed gobs playing with small maggotlike beggar-children. Pale-faced Levantines with slinking eyes and hooked noses. Armenians with querulous mouths and great gold brown eyes. In the bright sun and the violent shadows faces blur and merge as they pass. Faces are smooth and yellow like melons, steely like axes; faces are like winter squashes, like death's heads and jack o'lanterns and cocoanuts and sprouting potatoes. They merge slowly in the cruel white sunlight, brown faces under fezzes, yellow faces under straw-hats, pale northern faces under khaki caps—into one face, brows sullen and contracted, eyes black with suffering, skin taut over the cheekbones, hungry lines about the corners of the mouth, lips restless, envious, angry, lustful. The face of a man not quite starved out.

They are the notes, these faces, twanged on the trembling strings of this skein of frustrate lives that is Pera. So many threads out of the labyrinth. If one could only follow back into the steep dilapidated streets where the black wooden houses overhang, and women with thick ankles look down with kohl-smeared eyes at the porters who stumble under their huge loads up the uneven steps, sweating so that the red out of their fezzes runs in streaks down their knobbed and shaggy cheeks; through the sudden plane-shaded lanes that snatch occasional unbelievable blue distances of sea or umber distances of hills seen through the tilting and delicately-carved tombposts of Turkish cemeteries, and lead out into the pathless heaps of masonry of burnt-over places, where gapes an occasional caving dome with beside it a gnawed minaret, where sneakthieves and homeless people live in the remnants of houses or in shattered cisterns; or down through the waterfront streets of Galata with their fruitstands and their Greek women jiggling in doorways and their sailors' cafés full of the jingle of mechanical pianos or the brassy trombone music of an orchestra, where the dancing of ill-assorted closehugged couples has a sway of the sea to it; or through the cool bazaars of Stamboul where in the half darkness under the azure-decorated vault Persian and Greek and Jewish and Armenian merchants spread out print cloths and Manchester goods which an occasional beam of dusty sunlight sets into a flame of colors; or into the ruined palaces along the Bosphorus where refugees from one place or another live in dazed and closepacked squalor; or into the gorgeous tinsel-furnished apartments where Greek millionaires and Syrian war-profiteers give continual parties just off the Grande Rue de Pera; or to the yards and doorways where the Russians sleep huddled like sheep in a snowstorm: somewhere some day one might find the core, the key to decipher this intricate arabesque scrawled carelessly on a ground of sheer pain.

This afternoon I can only sit sipping douzico made opal white with water, ears drowsy with the strangely satisfying monotony of the Turkish orchestra's unending complaint. The cool north wind off the Black Sea has come up and is making dust and papers dance in whirlwinds across Taxim Square.

Along the line of taxis, abolishing them, abolishing the red trolleycars and the victorious puttees of Greek officers, his head in embroidered cap bowed against the wind, his almond eyes closed to black slits against the dust, taking little steps in his black embroidered slippers, the great sleeves of his flowing crimson silk gown flapping in the wind, walks a mandarin of China.

Cathay!

7. Constantine and the Classics

Little Mr. Moscoupoulos threw up pudgy hands.

—But the Turks have not studied the Greek classics. They are ignorant. They do not know Aristophanes or Homer or Demosthenes, not even the deputies. Et sans connaître les classiques grecs on ne peut être ni politicien, ni orateur, ni diplomate. Turkey does not exist. I assure you, sir, it is a mere question of brigandage. And this city—we peered out of the window of the Pera Palace at a passing Allied staffcar—you know the legend. A Constantine built it, a Constantine lost it, and a Constantine shall regain it. . . .

Overhead bunches of green grapes hang down from the dense thatch of vineleaves and twined stems. A café outside one of the gates in the great wall of Heraclius. The dusty road dips into a low gateway that seems too small for the heavy dust-raising carts that clatter through it. On either side grey square towers timecrumbled at the top. Endlessly in either direction, grey walls occasionally splotched with the bright green of a figtree, and grey square towers. Towards the east a patch of the luminous aquamarine blue of the Sea of Marmora; westward bare umber-colored hills. In the purplish shadow of the vine arbor little tables and stools of unpainted wood and on each table a pot of rosemary or basil or thyme or a geranium in flower. In a group in one corner old men with grave gestures discuss some problem with quietly modulated voices. Their white turbans are almost motionless; now and then there is a flash of white when a head nods in a patch of sun, or a hand, lean and brown, is lifted to a grey beard. Beside me three young men in fezzes of new bright red are exchanging witticisms. An old gentleman with a puffy red face, dressed in the eternal white vest and broadtailed frock coat, listens, looks across his narghile with eyes sparkling and occasionally throws his head back and roars with laughter. A yellow slender man with green carpet slippers beside him is looking into vacancy with large yellowbrown eyes, in his hand a long amber cigarette-holder that is bright gold when the sun strikes it.

Sans connaître les classiques on ne peut être ni diplomate, ni politicien, ni orateur. . . . But one can sit in the shade where the cool wind rustles the vineleaves, letting the days slip through the fingers smooth and decorously shaped as the lumps of amber of the conversation beads with which one hand or the other constantly plays.

Out of the gate snorting and grinding in low gear comes a staffcar full of Allied officers, glint of gold braid and a chattering of voices. A cloud of dust hides it as it crawls up the uneven road.

A flock of sheep forms bleating out of the dust, followed by two shepherds who shout and throw stones and beat with their sticks until the sheep begin to flow through the narrow gate like water through the outlet in a trough.

Sans connaître les classiques. . . . A party of the Inter-Allied police-force has come up and they stare searchingly in the faces of the Turks in the café. There are two Italian gendarmes with shiny threecornered hats and buttons on their coattails, some British M.P.s with hard red necks, French flics with the whiskers familiar to Paris cartoonists. They are all redfaced and sweaty from their rounds and there is dust on their highly polished shoes. When they have stared their fill at the people in the café they turn and go through the gate into town. Under the vines no one has noticed them. The voices of the old men continue, and the slow movement of a hand stroking a beard. In the upper bowl of the narghiles there is a little red glow at long intervals when the smoker pulls deeply. Above the grey towers and the wall, kites with black curved wings and hawk-beaks circle in the porcelain-blue sky.

8. ALEXANDERS

Going down to Therapia they pointed out the place where two nights before a French truck with a regimental fanfare in it had gone over the khud. Ah, monsieur, nous avons vécu des journées atroces, said the tall Greek lady beside me with a dangerous roll of her black eyes. At the next curve the car gave a terrible lurch to avoid an old man with a mule—Four of them were killed outright. They say they were dead drunk anyway. They never found the truck or the bodies . . . le Bosphore, vous comprenez. She smiled coyly with her large lips on which the rouge was restricted to a careful Cupid's bow.

At Therapia we sat on the terrace with the green swift Bosphorus in front of us and watched Englishmen in white flannels play tennis. A hot stagnant afternoon. Locusts whirred madly among the dusty cypresses. People in frock coats sat whispering round the little tables.

Mr. Deinos who was starting a steamship line to run from Constantinople to New York, sat in a lavender grey linen suit between the two tall ladies with lurching eyes and Cupid's-bow mouths coyly puckered. . . . Greece, he began, is going to fulfil her historic mission. . . .

I slipped away and strayed into the bar. A British major with a face like the harvest moon was shaking up Alexanders. A man in a frock coat was trying to catch in his mouth olives that an American relief worker was tossing in the air. The talk in the bar was English, Oxford drawl, Chicago burr, Yankee twang, English and American as spoken by Greeks, Armenians, Frenchmen, Italians. Only the soberer people in the corners spoke French.

—Intelligence service cleaned up another Bolo plot . . . yessiree. Collected all the Bolos in town and towed them up into the Black Sea in a leaky scow and left 'em there—Best place for them. Ungrateful beggars, these Russians. . . . Here we evacuate them from Odessa and Sebastopol and now they go turning red on us. The leader was a woman. . . . Picked her out of a room at the Tokatlian. When the A.P.C. knocked at the door she took off all her clothes and went to bed. Thought they'd be too gentlemanly to break in. Well they just wrapped her up in a blanket and carried her off the way she was.

—Well, sir, I was the last white man outa Sebastopol. . . . Agricultural machinery's my line.

—Turkish bandits carried off six Greeks last night from that village opposite. . . .

—Did you hear the one about young Stafford was walking with a Red Cross nurse out on the road near the Sweet Waters and bandits held them up? They didn't touch the girl but they stripped him down to the skin. . . . The girl made them give him back his drawers for decency.

—And the General said: There's not enough light, we want a flambeau in each of the windows. People tried to point out that the lace curtains might catch, but the General had had beaucoup champagne and kept calling for his flambeaux; well, they brought his flambeaux and the curtains did catch and now the Sultan has one less palace. . . . It was a great sight.

—This is extremely confidential, what I'm telling you now. This man we were talking about. His name begins with a Z. . . . You know the Vickers man. . . . You ask me some time about Vickers and the Ismid Roads. It seems that he's not a Jew at all but a Constantinople Greek. Everybody knew him around Pera, some little clothing business or other. Then one day he disappeared with the contents of a safe and turns up a couple of years later as a millionaire silk buyer in Lyon, and benefactor of the French Republic and all that sort of thing.

—No, this chap was a colonel on Wrangel's staff. They were starving and one day he found out that his wife and daughter had been . . . you know . . . for money and he shot 'em both dead and disappeared. Last night some charcoal burners found his body out in the hills. . . .

—Yessir I was the last white man outa Sebastopol . . . strange things you see in the Black Sea. . . . Agricultural machinery's my line. Last time I was out in Batum I seen upwards of six hundred women in swimmin' an' not one of 'em had a stitch on, in their birthday suits every one of 'em.

—Well, Major, how about another shakerful of Alexanders? They're mild and they hit the right spot.

—Kemal! He's finished. . . . Like hell he is. There's a lot of legendary stuff about him going round. How at Eski Chehir the Turkish army sank into the ground and came up behind the Greek lines. That's the kind of stuff that makes a hero in the east.

—They say that three divisions of Bolos are going in through Armenia and that he's promised 'em Constantinople in return for their help.

—Let 'em try and get it.

—They will get it some day.

—Nonsense the Greeks'll have it—The British—The French—The Bulgarians . . .—The League of Nations,—The Turks—I suggest it be made neutral and presented to Switzerland, that's the only solution.

Outside on the terrace Mr. Deinos and the two tall Greek ladies with Cupid's-bow mouths were eating pistachio nuts and drinking douzico in the amethyst twilight—Greece, continued Mr. Deinos, has always been the bulwark of civilization against the barbarians. Inspired by Marathon and Salamis and I hope by the help and sympathy of America, Greece is once more going to take up her historic mission. . . .

III. TREBIZOND

1. Afternoon Nap

Between Ineboli and Samsoun. Lying on the empty boat-deck of the Italian steamer *Aventino,* a scrawny boat that used to be Austrian, empty this trip except for several hundred Russian soldiers crowded into the forward hold, prisoners being repatriated. I'm lying on my face; through my shirt the two o'clock sun claws my back already stinging from the burn of a day's swimming at Prinkipo. In the space between the deck and the lifeboat I can sleepily see a great expanse of waves grey and green like the breast of a pigeon, and beyond the khaki hills of Asia Minor rising in enormous folds up to bloated white clouds that float in slaty reaches of mist. The wind stirs my hair and whispers in my ears; under my face the deck trembles warmly to the throb of the engines. There's no past and no future, only the drowsy, inexplicable surge of moving towards the sunrise across the rolling world. There's no opium so sweet as the unguarded sunny sleep on the deck of a boat when it's after lunch in summer and you don't know when you are going to arrive nor what port you will land at, when you've forgotten east and west and your name and your address and how much money you have in your pocket.

And then awake again looking up into the shimmering blue sky, thinking of Constant' and the interallied police strutting about and the bedbugs at the Pera Palace and long lines of ragged people waiting for visas for their passports, and the blue eyes of Russians, blue as the sky in sagged tallow faces; Russians standing at every corner selling papers and kewpie dolls, cigarettes, sugar buns, postcards, paper flowers, jumping jacks and jewelry; and the long-nosed Armenians sitting on squares of matting in the courtyards of falling down palaces, and the Turks from Macedonia sitting quiet under trees round the mosques in Stamboul, and the Greek refugees and the Jewish refugees and the charred streets of burnt-out bazaars; and late one night the onelegged man sobbing into his knotted hands.

Groggy with sleep and sun I got to my feet. Gulls were circling about the ship. Here the air was clean of misery and refugees and armies and police and passport officers. The Russian soldiers in the bow of the boat looked very happy. It was like looking down into a pit full of bear cubs. In their cramped quarters they played and wrestled and rolled each other about, big clumsy towheaded men in dirty tunics belted tight at the waist. They throw each other down with great bearlike swats, pick each other up laughing as if nothing could hurt them, kiss and start sparring again. They are restless like children kept in after school.

In a corner a bunch of Tatars squat gravely by themselves, broadfaced men with black slits for eyes. They sit motionless looking over the bright plain of the sea; a few of them play cards or cut up their bread in strips to dry it in the sun.

The captain, a tall man with white Umberto Primo whiskers, has come up gravely beside me and looks down into the hold, making a clucking noise with his tongue—They smell bad, those Russians. They have no officers. What's the use of sending them back just to make more Bolsheviki? I Alleati son' pazzi . . . tutti. They're crazy, the Allies, all of them. Aren't there enough Bolsheviki?

2. ANGORA

It was a surprise to find six Turkish army doctors in uniform sitting on the bench in the companionway. They certainly had been nowhere visible when we left Constantinople. They were worried about the Greek cruiser *Chilkis* that was sinking fishing boats and taking potshots at villages along the coast. They had the set faces of men with their backs to the wall. They treated me with jerky and very cold politeness.

—You Europeans are all hypocrites. When Turkish soldiers get out of hand and kill a few Armenians who are spies and traitors, you roll your eyes and cry massacre, but when the Greeks burn defenseless villages and murder poor fishermen it's making the world safe for democracy.

—I'm not a European, I'm an American.

—We believed your Meester Veelson. . . . All we want is to be left alone and reorganize our country in peace. If you believed in the rights of small nations why did you let the British set the Greeks on us? You think the Turk is an old man and sick, smoking a narghile. Perhaps we are old men and sick men, but originally we were nomads. We are sober and understand how to fight. If necessary we will become nomads again. If the Allies drive us out of Constantinople, very good. It is a city of misery and decay. We will make Angora our capital. We were not made to live in cities. Our life is in the fields and on the plains. If they drive us out of Angora we will go back to the great plains of central Asia, where we came from. Tell that to your high commissioners and your Meester Veelson. You have been to Stamboul. Did you see any Turks there? Only old people, beggars, Armenians and Jews, riffraff. The Turks are all in Angora with Mustapha Kemal.

—Are you going to Angora?

They nodded gravely—We are going to Angora.

3. Inexplicable Staircases

We are at anchor in the bay in front of Trebizond. I wear out the upper deck walking up and down. The authorities won't let any one ashore, as the *Ckilkis* shelled the town this morning. There's a rumor that they are carrying out reprisals on the remaining Greeks and Armenians, so I wear out the upper deck and stare at the town till my eyes are ready to pop out of my head.

A pink and white town built on arches, terracing up among

cypresses, domes and minarets and weather-gnawed towers against a mother-of-pearl sky piling up over the shoulder of a bulky escarped hill. Further along, dull vermilion cliffs zigzagged with inexplicable white staircases climbing up from the sea and stopping suddenly in the face of the cliff.

Black luggers are coming out over the grassgreen water to unload the cargo.

Trebizond, one of the capitals of my childhood geography, a place of swords and nightingales and a purple-born princess in a garden where the trees grew rubies and diamonds instead of flowers, a lonely never-to-be-rescued princess bright and cold and slender as an icicle, guarded by gold lions and automaton knights and a spray of molten lead and roar and smoke of Greek fire.

And what is happening in this Trebizond under the white mask of walls and domes? There's no smoke from any of the houses, no sound comes across the water. I walk up and down wearing out the upper deck wondering at the white staircases that zigzag up from the sea and stop suddenly in the face of the cliff.

At sunset we hove anchor and started nudging down the coast into the gloom eastward.

IV. RED CAUCASUS

1. The Twilight of Things

Behind a cracked windowpane mended with tapes of paper, Things sit in forlorn conclave. In the center is the swagbellied shine of a big samovar, dented a little, the whistle on top askew, dust in the mouldings of the handles. Under it, scattered over a bit of mothchewed black velvet two silver Georgian sword-scabbards, some silver cups chased with a spinning sinewy pattern, a cracked carafe full of mould, some watches, two of them Swiss in tarnished huntingcases, one an Ingersoll, quite new, with an illuminated dial, several thick antique repeaters, a pair of Dresden candlesticks, some lace, a pile of cubes of cheap soap, spools of thread, packets of pins. Back in the shop a yellowfaced old man droops over a counter on which are a few bolts of printed calicos. Along the walls are an elaborate Turkish tabouret inlaid with mother-of-pearl, a mahogany dressing table without its mirror, and some iron washstands. The wrinkles have gathered into a deep cleft between the old man's brows; his eyes have the furtive snarl of a dog disturbed on a garbage pile. He looks out through narrowed pupils at the sunny littered street, where leanfaced men sit with their heads in their hands along the irregular curb, and an occasional drovshky goes by pulled by bony racks of horses, where soldiers loaf in doorways.

The old man is the last guardian of Things. Here possessions, portable objects, personal effects, Things, that have been the goal and prize of life, the great center of all effort, to be sweated for and striven for and cheated for by all generations, have somehow lost their import and crumbled away and been trampled underfoot. The people who limp hungrily along the rough-paved streets never look in the windows of the speculators' shops, never stop to look enviously at the objects that perhaps they once owned. They seem to have forgotten Things.

Only an occasional foreigner off a steamer in the harbor goes into the old man's shop, to haggle for this trinket or that, to buy jewels to resell in Europe, or in back rooms behind locked doors to paw over furs or rugs that can be smuggled out of the country only after endless chaffering and small bribery. The boat the night before we got to Batum was full of talk of this and that which might be picked up for nothing, pour un rien, per piccolo prezzo. People scrubbed up their wits, overhauled their ways and means, like fishermen their tackle the night before the opening of the trout season.

As one glances into the houses strolling through the tree-shaded streets of Batum one sees mostly high empty rooms, here and there a bed or a table, some cooking utensils, a scrap of mosquito-netting or a lace curtain across an open window. All the intricate paraphernalia, all the small shiny and fuzzy and tasseled objects that padded the walls of existence have melted away. Perhaps most of them went in the war under the grinding wheels of so many invading and occupying armies, the Russians, the Germans, the British, the Turks, the Georgian Social-Democrats and lastly the Red Army. After these years of constant snatching and pillage, of frequent terrified trundling of cherished objects into hiding-places, seems to have come apathy. People lie all day on the pebbly beach in front of the town, with their rags stripped off them, baking in the sun, now and then dipping into the long green swells that roll off the Black Sea, or sit chatting in groups under the palms of the curious higgledy-piggledy Elysium of the Boulevard along the waterfront. With half-starvation has come a quiet effortlessness probably sweeter than one might expect, something like the delicious sleep they say drugs men who are freezing to death.

And the poor remnants of what people persist in calling civilization lie huddled and tarnished and dusty in the windows of second-hand dealers, Things useful and useless, well made and clumsily made, and little by little they are wafted away west in return for dollars and lire and English pounds and Turkish pounds that lie in the hoards with which the dealers, the men with the eyes of dogs frightened on a garbage pile, await the second coming of their Lord.

2. THE KNIGHT OF THE PANTHERSKIN

There is a bright sliver of the moon in the sky. On the horizon of a sea sheening green and bright lilac like the breast of a pigeon a huge sun swells red to bursting. Palmfronds and broad leaves of planes sway against a darkening zenith. In the space of dust outside of their barracks Georgian soldiers are gathered lazily into a circle. They wear ragged greyish uniforms, some with round fur caps, some with the pointed felt helmets of the Red Army. Many of them are barefoot. Blows off them a sweaty discouraged underfed smell. One man, seated, starts thumping with his palms a double shuffle on a small kettledrum held between his legs. The rest beat time by clapping until one man breaks out into a frail melody. He stops at the end of a couple of phrases, and a young fellow, blond, rather sprucely dressed with a clean white fur cap on the back of his head, starts dancing. The rest keep time with their hands and sing Tra-la-la, Tra-la-la to the tune in a crooning undertone. The dance is elegant, mincing, with turkeylike struttings and swift hunting gestures, something in it of the elaborate slightly farded romance of eastern chivalry. One can imagine silver swords and spangled wallets and gaudy silk belts with encrusted buckles. Perhaps it is a memory that makes the men's eyes gleam so as they beat time, a memory of fine horses and long inlaid guns and toasts drunk endlessly out of drinking horns, and of other more rousing songs sung in the mountains at night of the doughty doings of the Knight of the Pantherskin.

3. PROLETCULT

On the walls some crude squares of painting in black and white, a man with a pick, a man with a shovel, a man with a gun. The shadows are so exaggerated they look like gingerbread men. Certainly the man who painted them had not done many figures before in his life. The theater is a long tin shed that used to be a cabaret show of some sort, the audience mostly workmen and soldiers in white tunics open at the neck, and women in white muslin dresses. Many of the men and all the children are barefoot and few of the women wear stockings. When the curtain goes up romping and chattering stop immediately; everyone is afraid of missing a word of what is said on the stage. It's a foolish enough play, an Early-Victorian sob-story, about a blind girl and a good brother and a wicked brother, and a bad marquis and a frequently fainting marquise, but the young people who play it—none of them ever acted before the Red Army entered Batum three months ago—put such conviction into it that one can't quite hold aloof from the very audible emotion of the audience during the ticklish moments of the dagger-fight between the frail good brother and the wicked and hearty elder brother who has carried off the little blind girl against her will. And when at last all wrongs are righted, and the final curtain falls on felicity, one can't help but feel that the lives of these people who crowd out through the dilapidated ex-beergarden in front of the theater have somehow been compensated for the bareness of the hungry livingrooms and barracks they go home to. In the stamping and the abandon with which the two heroes fought was perhaps an atom of some untrammelled expression, of some gaudy bloodcurdling ritual which might perhaps replace in people's hopes and lives the ruined dynasty of Things.

4. BEES

The secretary of the commission for schools recently set up in Batum was a blackhaired man, hawknosed, hollow-eyed, with a three-day growth of beard. Undernourishment and overwork had made his eyes a little bloodshot and given them a curious intense stare. He had a sheaf of papers in front of him among which he scribbled an occasional hasty word, as if pressed for time. He spoke French with difficulty, digging it up word by word from some long-forgotten layer of his mind. He talked about the new school-system the Bolsheviki were introducing in the new republic of Adjaria, of which Batum was the capital, explained how already children's summer colonies had been started in several villages, how every effort was being made to get equipment ready to open the primary and secondary schools at the end of September.

—All education is to be by work, nothing without actual touch; he spread his hands, that were angular tortured painful hands, wide, and closed them with a gesture of laying hold onto some slippery reality. The words he used, too, were concrete, dug out of the soil—From the very first, work. . . . In summer in the fields, the children must cultivate gardens, raise rabbits, bees, chickens, learn how to take care of cattle. They must go into the forests and learn about trees. Everything they must learn by touch. Then in the winter they must study their native languages and Esperanto. . . . Here there will be schools for Armenians, Greeks, Muslims, Georgians, Russians . . . and the rudiments of sociology, arithmetic, woodworking, cooking. For in our republic every man must be able to attend to his wants himself. That will be the primary education. You see, nothing by theory, everything by practice. Then the secondary education will be more specialized, preparation for trades and occupations. Then those who finish the high schools can go to the universities to do independent work in the directions they have chosen. You see, merit will be according to work, not by theories or examinations. And all through there will be instruction in music and gymnastics and the theater; the arts must be open to anyone who wants to work in them. But most important will be nature; the young children must be all the time in the fields and forests, among the orchards where there are bees. . . . It is in the little children that all our hope lies . . . among orchards where there are bees.

32

5. Bedbug Express

Ce n'est pas serios, the tall Swede had said when he and I and an extremely evil-looking Levantine with gimlet-pointed whiskers had not been allowed to go down the gangplank at Batum. Ce n'est pas serios, he had said, indicating the rotting harbor and the long roofs of the grey and black town set in dense pyrites-green trees and the blue and purple mountains in the distance and the Red Guards loafing on the wharf and the hammer and sickle of the Soviet Republic painted on the wharfhouse. The last I saw of him he was still standing at the end of the gangplank, the points of his standup collar making pink dents in his thick chin, shaking his head and muttering, Ce n'est pas serios.

I thought of him when, accompanied by a swaggering interpreter and by a cheerful man very worried about typhus from the N.E.R., I stood in front of the Tiflis express waving a sheaf of little papers in my hand, passes in Georgian and in Russian, transport orders, sleeping car tickets, a pass from the Cheka and one from the Commissar for Foreign Affairs of the Republic of Adjaria. The Tiflis express consisted of an engine, three huge unpainted sleepers and a very gaudy suncracked caboose. One car was reserved for civil officials, one for the military and one for the general public. So far it was extremely serious, but the trouble was that long before the train had drawn into the station it had been stormed by upwards of seven thousand people, soldiers in white tunics, peasant women with bundles, men with long moustaches and astrakhan caps, speculators with peddlers' packs and honest proletarians with loaves of bread, so that clots of people all sweating and laughing and shoving and wriggling obliterated the cars, like flies on a lump of sugar. There were people on every speck of the roof, people hanging in clusters from all the doors, people on the coal in the coalcar, people on the engine; from every window protruded legs of people trying to wriggle in. Those already on board tried to barricade themselves in the compartments and with surprising gentleness tried to push the newcomers out of the windows again. Meanwhile the eastbound American ran up and down the platform dragging his hippopotamus suitcase, streaking sweat from every pore and trying to find a chink to hide himself in. At last recourse had to be had to authority. Authority gave him a great boost by the seat of the pants that shot him and his suitcase in by a window into a compartment full of very tall men in very large boots, six of the seven soldiers who occupied his seat were thrown out, all hands got settled and furbished up their foreign languages and sat quietly sweating waiting for the train to leave.

Eventually after considerable circulation of rumors that we were not going to leave that day, that the track was torn up, that a green army had captured Tiflis, that traffic was stopped on account of the cholera, we started off without the formality of a whistle. The train wound slowly through the rich jade and emerald jungle of the Black Sea coast towards tall mountains to the northeast that took on inconceivable peacock colors as the day declined. In the compartment we nibbled black bread and I tried to juggle French and German into a conversation. Someone was complaining of the lack of manufactured articles, paint and women's stockings and medicine and spare parts for automobiles and soap and flatirons and toothbrushes. Someone else was saying that none of those things were necessary: The mountains will give us wool, the fields will give us food, the forests will give us houses; let every man bake his own and spin his own and build his own; that way we will be happy and independent of the world. If only they would not compromise with industrialism. But in Moscow they think, if only we get enough foreign machinery the revolution will be saved; we should be self-sufficient like the bees.

Strange how often they speak to you of bees. The order and sweetness of a hive seem to have made a great impression on the Russians of this age. Again and again in Tiflis people talked of bees with a sort of wistful affection, as if the cool pungence of bees were a tonic to them in the midst of the soggy bleeding chaos of civil war and revolution.

By this time it was night. The train was joggling its desultory way through mountain passes under a sky solidly massed with stars like a field of daisies. In the crowded compartment, where people had taken off their boots and laid their heads on each other's shoulders to sleep, hordes of bedbugs had come out of the stripped seats and bunks, marching in columns of three or four, well disciplined and eager. I had already put a newspaper down and sprinkled insect powder in the corner of the upper berth in which I was hemmed by a solid mass of sleepers. The bedbugs took the insect powder like snuff and found it very stimulating, but it got into my nose and burned, got into my eyes and blinded me, got into my throat and choked me, until the only thing for it was to climb into the baggage rack, which fortunately is very large and strong in the Brobdignagian Russian trains. There I hung, eaten only by the more acrobatic of the bugs, the rail cutting into my back, the insect powder poisoning every breath, trying to make myself believe that a roving life was the life for me. Above my head I could hear the people on the roof stirring about.

At about midnight the train stopped for a long while at a station. Tea was handed round, made in great samovars like watertanks; their fires were the only light; you could feel that there was a river below in the valley, a smell of dry walls and human filth came up from some town or other. Huge rounded shoulders of hills cut into the stars. Enlivened by the scalding tea, we all crawled into our holes again, the bunches of people holding on at the doors reformed, and the train was off. This time I went very decently to sleep listening to the stirring of the people on the roof above my head, to the sonorous rumble of the broad-gauge wheels and to a concertina that wheezed out a torn bit of song now and then in another car.

In the morning we look out at a silver looping river far below in a huge valley between swelling lioncolored hills. The train casts a strange shadow in the morning light, all its angles obliterated by joggling, dangling figures of soldiers; on the roofs are the shadows of old women with baskets, of men standing up and stretching themselves, of children with caps too big for them. On a siding we pass the long train of the second tank division of the Red Army; a newpainted engine, then endless boxcars, blond young soldiers lolling in the doors. Few of them look more than eighteen; they are barefoot and scantily dressed in canvas trousers and tunics; they look happy and at their ease, dangling their legs from the roofs and steps of boxcars and sleepers. You can't tell which are the officers. Out of the big clubcar decorated with signs and posters that looks as if it might have been a diner in its day, boys lean to wave at the passing train. Then come flatcars with equipment, then a long row of tanks splotched and striped with lizard green—A gift of the British, says the man beside me. The British gave them to Denikin, and Denikin left them to us.

Our train, the windows full of travelgrimed faces and the seats full of vermin, gathers speed and tilts round a bend. The sight of the green tanks has made everybody feel better. The man beside me, who used to be a banker in Batum and hopes to be again, exclaims fervently: All these words, Bolshevik, Socialist, Menshevik, have no meaning any more. . . . Conscious of it or not, we are only Russians.

6. The Relievers

Members of the N.E.R. sign a pledge not to drink fermented or distilled liquors. A private car full of members of the N.E.R. is in Tiflis trying to decide whether starving people or people with full bellies are more likely to become communists. In Tiflis twenty people a day die of cholera, forty people a day die of typhus, not counting those who die where nobody finds them. At the N.E.R. headquarters we all sleep on canvas cots and gargle with listerine to avoid infection and to take the vodka off our breaths. Headquarters swarms with miserable barons and countesses who naturally sigh for the old régime and color the attitude of even the honest men among the relievers. What American can stand up against a title, much less against a refugee title in distress? Why, she might be the Princess Anastasia in disguise! The Russian government understands all that but wisely argues that a live White child is better than a dead Red child; so it gives the relievers a free hand to decide what sheep shall live and what goats shall die.

But the real energy of the relievers goes into the relief of Things. To a casual eye Tiflis is bare of Things, nothing in the shopwindows, houses empty as the tents of arabs, but towards the N.E.R. there is a constant streaming of diamonds, emeralds, rubies, silver-encrusted daggers, rugs, Georgian, Anatolian, rugs from Persia and Turkestan, watches, filigree work, silver mesh bags, furs, amber, the Mustapha Sirdar papers, cameras, fountain pens. My dear, the bargains! For a suitcase full of roubles you can outfit yourself for life. I guess the folks back home'll be surprised when I tell 'em what I paid for that sunburst I bought the wife.

And, carrying the things, greyfaced people, old men and women terribly afraid of the Cheka of brigands of the cholera, of their shadows, débris of a wrecked world, selling for a few days' food, Things that had been the mainstay of their lives up to 1917; swaggering young men who had picked the winning team and were making a good thing of it; professional speculators, men who were usually but not always Greeks, Armenians, or Jews, men with sharp eyes and buzzard beaks, dressed in shabby overcoats, humpbacked with respect and politeness, rubbing their hands that never let go a banknote however depreciated the currency was, men who will be the founders of great banking houses in the future, philanthropists and the founders of international families. The bargains, the bargains!

And the pride and virtue of the members of the N.E.R. who had signed a pledge not to drink alcoholic or fermented liquors, who are relieving the sufferings of humanity at the risk of their lives, who are exposing themselves to the contamination of Bolshevism, communism, free love, nationalized women, anarchy and God knows what— their virtuous pride in the dollar king of the exchange as they paw over the bargains; rugs stolen out of the mosques, lamps out of churches; pearls off the neck of a slaughtered grand duchess; the fur coat of some poor old woman who sits hungry in her bare room looking out through a chink in the shutters at this terrible young people's world, a world jagged and passionate and crude that she can never understand, an old woman looking out through the shutters with the eyes of a cat that has been run over by an automobile.

7. Funicular

The inevitable Belgian Company still runs the funicular. You pay your fare to a little Polish girl neat as a mouse in a white dress. On her legs a faint ruddiness of sunburn takes the place of stockings. She complains of the lack of talcum powder and stockings and wonders what she's going to do when her shoes wear out. The car creaks jerkily up the hill. Above the shelter of the town a huge continual wind is blowing.

Back from a walk over the hills, I sit at a table outside a little shanty, drinking a bottle of wine of Kakhetia no. 66. Old Tiflis, dust-colored with an occasional patch of blue or white on a house, is loosely sprinkled in the funnel out of which the copper-wire river pours into the plain. Out of the defile rises a column of steam from the sulphur springs. Farther down, the enormous grey buildings of the Russian town straggle over the plain. From the valley bulge row after row of vast stratified hills, ochre and olivecolor, that get blue into the distance until they break into the tall range of the Caucasus barring the north. The huge continual streaming wind out of Asia, a wind so hard you can almost see it streaked like marble, a wind of unimaginable expanses, whines in the mouth of my glass and tears to tatters the insane jig that comes out of the mechanical piano behind me. I have to hold the bottle between my knees to keep it from blowing over.

We used to dream of a wind out of Asia that would blow our cities clean of the Things that are our gods, the knick-knacks and the scraps of engraved paper and the vases and the curtain rods, the fussy junk possession of which divides poor man from rich man, the shoddy manufactured goods that are all our civilization prizes, that we wear our hands and brains out working for; so that from being an erect naked biped, man has become a sort of hermit crab that can't live without a dense conglomerate shell of dinnercoats and limousines and percolators and cigarstore coupons and eggbeaters and sewing machines, so that the denser his shell, the feebler his self-sufficience, the more he is regarded a great man and a millionaire. That wind has blown Russia clean, so that the Things held divine a few years ago are mouldering rubbish in odd corners; thousands of lives have been given and taken (from where I sit I can make out the square buildings of the Cheka, crammed at this minute with poor devils caught in the cogs) a generation levelled like gravel under a steamroller to break the tyranny of Things, goods, necessities, industrial civilization. Just now it's the lull after the fight. The gods and devils are taking their revenge on the victors with cholera and famine. Will the result be the same old piling up of miseries again, or a faith and a lot of words like Islam or

Christianity, or will it be something impossible, new, unthought of, a life bare and vigorous without being savage, a life naked and godless where goods and institutions will be broken to fit men, instead of men being ground down fine and sifted in the service of Things?

Harder, harder blows the wind out of Asia; it has upset the table, taken the chair out from under me. Bottle in one hand, glass in the other, I brace myself against the scaring wind.

8. INTERNATIONAL

The eastbound American had dinner of caviar and tomatoes and Grusinski shashlik and watermelon washed down with the noble wine of Kakhetia in the pleasant gone-to-seed Jardin des Petits Champs, where nobody thinks of cholera or typhus or the famine along the Volga. Afterwards strolling through unlit streets, you met no old people, only crowds of young men in tunics and dark canvas trousers, some of them barefoot, young girls in trim neatly cut white dresses without stockings or hats, strolling happily in threes and fours and groups, filling the broad empty asphalt streets.

The night was warm and a dry wind drove the dust. The Grusinski garden, that used to be the Noblemen's Club, was crowded with the new softly laughing youngsters. A band was playing Light Cavalry. A few colored electric bulbs hung among the waving trees. There was nothing particular to do. In spite of famine and cholera and typhus everybody seemed nonchalant and effortlessly gay. A certain amount of wine was being sold, illegally, I think, at a table in a corner, but nobody but the Americans seemed to have any roubles to buy it with. Gradually the crowd was trickling into a theater that had great signs in Russian and in Georgian over the door. The eastbound American found himself in a narrow corridor being addressed as Amerikanski Poait and before he knew what was happening he found himself being settled in a seat in a curiously shaped room; as he was reaching for someone who spoke a known language one wall of the room rose and he found that he was on a stage facing an enormous auditorium packed with people. In the front row were broad grins on the faces of certain companions he had been with earlier in the evening. Then somebody behind his chair whispered in French into his ear that it was an international proletarian poetry festival and that he was expected to recite something. At that news the E. A. almost fainted.

The proceedings were splendid. Not more than ten people present ever understood any one thing. Poems were recited, chanted and sung in Armenian, Georgian, Turkish, Persian, Russian, German and God knows what else. Everything was received with the greatest enthusiasm. The E. A. managed to stammer out as his own a nursery rhyme by William Blake, the only thing he could remember, which revolutionary outburst was received with cheers. The E. A. retired in confusion and in a muck of sweat, feeling that probably he had mistaken his vocation. Certainly *Oh Sunflower weary of time* can never have been recited under stranger conditions. After a long poem in Russian by a thin young soldier with a conical head shaved bald that made everybody roar with laughter until the building shook, the meeting broke up amid the greatest international merriment and singing and everybody started streaming home through the pitchblack streets, young men in white tunics, bareheaded girls in white dresses, strolling about without restraint in this empty world like children playing in an abandoned house, gradually swallowed up by the huge black barracklike buildings.

On the way up the hill we passed the Cheka. The pavements round it were brilliantly lit. There was barbed wire in the windows. Sentries walked back and forth. As we walked past, trying to close our nostrils to the jail smell, the idyll crashed about our ears.

Up at the N.E.R. there was considerable excitement. One of the relievers was with difficulty being got into his cot. Others were talking about typhus and cholera. One man was walking round showing everyone a handful of heavy silver soupspoons—Five cents apiece in American money, what do you think of that?—Are you sure they're not plated?—Genuine English sterling silver marked with the lion; can't get anything better'n that—Because Major Vokes bought a necklace in Batum and it turned out to be paste.

I lay curled up on my cot listening to all this from the next room; the uneasy smell of the summer night came in through the open window with a sliver of moonlight. The street outside was empty and dark, but frailly from far away came the sound of a concertina. The jiggly splintered tune of a concertina was limping its way through the black half desert stone city, slipping in at the windows of barracks, frightening the middleaged people who sat among the last of their Things trembling behind closed shutters, maddening the poor devils imprisoned in the basement of the Cheka, caught under the wheels of the juggernaut of revolution, as people are caught under the wheels in every movement forward or back of the steamroller of human action. The jail is the cornerstone of liberty, thought the E. A. as he fell asleep.

V. ONE HUNDRED VIEWS OF ARARAT

1. TIFLIS

The train was made up of one small passenger car jammed with soldiers and many boxcars. I sat on my bag on the station platform as it pulled in and stared ruefully at the grandiloquent order for a compartment in the sleeping-car they had given me at the office of the Commissar for Foreign Affairs. The usual ragged crowd that haunts all railway stations in the Caucasus was scuttling up and down, dragging bags and gunnysacks from one side to the other, a sweating threadbare medley of peasants and soldiers. The Sayyid (that means descendant of the Prophet or of Ali, son of Abu Talib) strode about and made a great speech in Persian and Turkish to everyone who would listen on the rights and appurtenances of a diplomatic passport. At last, after much prodding of a weary interpreter and seeing of dignitaries at desks, it was decided that the nearest equivalent to a sleeper would be the freightcar that carried the newspapers and that the instructive company of great bundles of the *Isvestia* and the *Pravda* would be even superior to a compartment and a berth, that was, if the Commissar in charge consented. More commissars at desks were interviewed. Of course the Commissar was only too delighted. . . . The car was opened and one Samsoun, an Armenian, was discovered therein, to whom the Sayyid addressed a fervent allocation in Turkish on the virtues of cleanliness and hygiene, with the result that water was brought and lysol splashed to the very roof and new copies of all of Moscow's most famous newspapers spread on the floor for us to sit on. At that point the Sayyid drew his knife and began to massacre a watermelon, and Samsoun effendi, or more properly Tavarishch Samsoun began to make a lustful gurgling noise in his thoat and brazenly asked for cognac. We put him off with a promise of wine later and with a slice of melon. At that point the two grimy youths who were Samsoun's underlings climbed aboard and the train, late only by some five hours, rumbled out of the station.

A curious sort of existence people lead along the railroad tracks in the Caucasus and, I suppose, all over Russia; the dilapidated arteries of communication exercise an uneasy sort of attraction. In all the stations there are crowds and even at crossings that seem very far from any village, groups of men and women stand and watch the train go by. Perhaps they feel a vague ownership over the endless gleaming rails and the oilsmeared locomotives, feel that somehow by this means their hungry frustrate lives are linked to great happenings far away. Then so many people seem to live all their lives along the tracks. The soldiers of the Red Army are in many cases permanently quartered in passengercars and freightcars fitted up with bunks that fill up all the sidings joined in long trains with staffcars and clubcars and hospitalcars and with cars loaded with the black bread and salt herring that form the staple rations. Then there are the special armored trains that have been one of the features of each of the campaigns of the civil war. Furthermore, particularly near towns, there are hundreds of freightcars fitted up with windows and stovepipes, used as houses by all manner of families—refugees from Lord knows where, people who repair the railroad, minor officials, gypsies, vagabonds of all sorts. And as the train goes by all this population cranes from between sliding doors and from the little windows of cabooses and scrutinizes with mild insolence the soldiers and peasants and civil employees who sprawl on the roofs and dangle their legs from the open doors of jerkily moving boxcars.

2. Karakliss

Moonlight sifts through tall poplars by the railway track and mingles strangely on the floor of the boxcar with the glimmer of the candle in my corner. The Sayyid has contrived a sort of bed out of his suitcase and the provision box and is somewhat uneasily asleep. Probably he's dreaming of Pan-Islam and driving off the attacks of hundreds of little British devils with cloven hoofs and pith helmets. At the other end of the car the Georgian and Samsoun and his myrmidons have made beds for themselves among the piles of newspapers. Outside, the station platform is deserted, drowned in moonlight. There is the sound of a stream. All along the picket fence are the shadows of people asleep. Along with the clean smell of the river and the mountains that rear spiny backs into the sheer moonlight behind the poplars, comes occasionally a miserable disheartening stench of cold sweat and rags and filthy undernourished bodies huddled somewhere in the sheds about the station.

Ever since sunset we've been in Armenia, having crossed the neutral zone where the Georgians and Armenians burnt each other's villages till the British stopped them, back in 1918. At the last Georgian stations before we started to climb this long valley up into the Little Caucasus everybody on the train invested largely in watermelons, which could be bought for a couple of thousand roubles apiece. Up here in the mountains and in the famine area, they sell for ten thousand or more.

At about dusk we had great excitement. Shots were fired and whistles blown all down the train. Samsoun effendi drew an enormous revolver and began to whirl it about with great heroism, and sent off the smallest boy to find out what was the matter. First the news came that a woman had fallen off the top of a freightcar and been killed, but it eventually transpired that it was only a bag of flour that had fallen out of the American relief car. So the flour was picked up and everybody got back to his place, in the cars or on the roof or on the rods, and the train started wheezing its way up the grade again. Samsoun effendi was put in high spirits by the accident and started telling us of past deeds of valor, pointing the revolver absentmindedly at each person in turn as he did so. To get the revolver back into its holster the Sayyid and I had to crack a bottle of our best wine of Kakhetia. The effect was magical. The smallest youngster, a curious boy with a face as careworn as a monkey's, began to sing songs of the Volga in an unexpectedly deep voice. The Georgian tightened his belt and slapped his thighs and began to dance, and a broad grin divided the rugged features, partly like those of a camel and partly like those of the Terrible Turk of the cartoons, of Samsoun effendi himself.

3. ALEXANDROPOL

Dusty soldiers and freightyards jammed with freightcars of which the paint has peeled under the hot sun. The little Armenian girl has picked up her basket and gone. She appeared somewhere in the night in tow of a white-whiskered station master. Caused quite a stir. The Sayyid sat up on his valise, and noticing that she had on her chin the mole so admired of Orientals, put on an air of the most splendid doggishness and cried out Quel théâtre! in a loud voice. Samsoun effendi lit a candle and started smoothing his hair, looking at himself with great satisfaction in a small pocket mirror the while. But the Armenian girl was quite unmoved by all these manifestations and went calmly to sleep with her head on her basket.

As it grew light we crossed the watershed of the Little Caucasus. On the north side the villages, scattered collections of square houses of volcanic stone, roofed with turf and often topped by tall hayricks, were intact, and wellfed peasants were already in the fields getting in the crops, but from the moment the train started winding down the southerly slope, everything was sheer desert. The last Turkish attack, in 1920, had wiped the country clean; not a house intact in the villages, no crops, even the station buildings systematically destroyed, and everything movable carted away. Ghengiz Khan and his Tatars couldn't have laid waste more thoroughly. Alexandropol itself, though war-seedy to the last degree, had evidently been spared. It straggles among railway yards on a yellow scorched plain, where the wind blows the dust in swirling clouds from one side to the other;

the most outstanding buildings are the great rows of grey barracks where orphans are housed by the Near East Relief. On the station platform the usual crowd, ragged peasants and soldiers, Russian and Armenian.

Ararat, when I first saw it, was as faintly etched against a grey sky as is Fuji in some of Hokusai's Hundred Views, a tall cone streaked white against pearly mist. The train was winding round a shoulder of the hills through reddish badlands that glistened in the flat spaces with alkali. Some time before the Georgian had pointed up over dry hills and said—Ani. Somewhere in the rocky wilderness to our left there had been the capital of the ancient kingdom of Armenia. I was as excited at the sight of Ararat as if I could see the Ark still balanced on the peak of it, and made an attempt to stir the Sayyid's enthusiasm on the subject. But he refused to budge from where he was tending an elaborate engine of sticks and bits of twine that was intended to keep the tiny teapot from falling off our tinier alcohol lamp. When he did finally get to his feet, he looked at the mountain appraisingly for a long time, taking little sips from a tin cup of tea, and then shook his head and said:—Damavand is higher and more pointed—But the Ark and Noah and the elephant and the kangaroo and all the rest of the zoo didn't land on Damavand!—They used to say that there were divs on Damavand, said the Sayyid, and considering the argument to have been brought to a satisfactory conclusion, he squatted in his corner again and began brewing a new pot of tea.

We were coming down from the hills into an irregular basinlike valley at the end of which the streaky white peak of Ararat soared on two great strongly-etched curves above the bluish mass of the mountain. In the foreground for a moment were the roofless stone walls of a village; from behind one of the huts drifted up a little woodsmoke from a campfire, but nowhere in the whole landscape of tortured hills and livid white alkali plains was anything alive to be seen. Then a squall that for a long time had been gathering up indigo fringes above the mountains to the west swept across and hid everything in oblique sheets of rain and hail.

At a station on the plain we sent Samsoun effendi to get water for tea, and instead he brought back, to the Sayyid's extraordinary delight, what the Sayyid always calls a Mademoiselle.

We sat on the mysterious packing case and looked out over the plains at Ararat, that now, much nearer, stood erect and luminous above the dusk that was already seeping into the plain. We had given the Mademoiselle a cup of tea and some black bread and caviar from our provision box, and she seemed vaguely content and expansive, like a cat tickled about the ears. Evidently she had been taut on the defensive all the journey. She had come from Tiflis in a car full of soldiers. She had a pleasant Teutonic face, with rounded cheeks and steel-blue eyes, like Vermeer's women, and was dressed with a faint reminiscence of style in a soiled white suit. She wore stockings, a distinction in these parts, and little rope sandals. She started to talk gradually, remembering her French with effort—Yes, I am going to Erivan. I work there as a stenographer in an office. . . . Of course a government office; there are no others. No, things aren't so bad there. People are starving. . . . Certainly it's worse than Tiflis, but, do you know? we are so used to it all now. We don't notice those things any more. We have a nice house and roses in the garden and I have dogs. . . . I even take horseback rides. Still, it's a miserable existence, and all because my father and mother took fright when the Germans were getting near to Riga. You see we are Esthonians, not Russians. We lived in Riga, and when it seemed as if the Germans would bombard the town we fled into Russia. Many other people fled, too. And then our troubles began—She laughed—What a time we live in!

The train had stopped at a station. The plain was marshy now. In front of us, beyond a canebrake, was Ararat, at the base indigo, cut across by level streaks of mist, and on the summit bright rose. Behind it like a shadow was the smaller cone, all dark, of Little Ararat. Mosquitoes whined in swarms about our ears.

—But as I was telling you, went on the mademoiselle,—oh, these mosquitoes! You can't live a week in Erivan without coming down with malaria; really it's a frightful place. . . . Everybody there is dying. . . . But anyway, although I was just a child then—you see I'm not awfully old now—I kept begging mother and father not to go. We had such a lovely big old house with linden trees round it and a garden full of overgrown shrubs where I used to play. You've never been in Riga? The Baltic is so beautiful in summer out among the islands. . . . My grandmother wouldn't leave. I think she's still alive, living in our old house. I'm going back there if I die in the attempt. . . . I have already applied for a passport, and I have seen the Esthonian consul in Tiflis. . . . That's what I went up for. But it's so difficult to get anything done here. They get so in the habit of prohibiting—She laughed again—Oh, they make me so angry. They just go about and if they find anybody wants to do anything, they cry: Stop it, stop it.

The Sayyid in his corner was boiling a new pot of water for tea. A lurch of the train upset pot and lamp and everything, so I left the mysterious packing case to help reconstruct the scaffolding on which depended the frequency of our cups of tea. A moment later I saw that Samsoun effendi, who had been at his little pocket mirror again, had taken my place and was deep in conversation with the Mademoiselle. She looked at me over his shoulder and wrinkling up her nose like a rabbit's, said: Il me fait la cour. Pensez!

The Sayyid looked from one to the other and suddenly let out a stentorian: Quel théâtre! Then laughing he reached for the last watermelon, sliced it deftly with his penknife, and handed me half of it as a peace-offering.

Through the little upper window of the boxcar I caught a last glimpse of Ararat for that day, as I sat on my suitcase with my teeth in the sweet dripping melon, three streaks of watermelon pink converging against a sky of solid indigo.

4. ERIVAN

Long straight grassgrown streets full of a sickly stench of dung and ditchwater. Half-naked children with the sagging cheeks and swollen bellies of starvation cower like hurt animals in doorways and recesses in the walls. Over grey walls here and there an appletree with fruit on it. Up above, the unflecked turquoise of the sky in which from every little eminence one can see the aloof white glitter of Ararat. They say, though I haven't seen it, that a dead wagon goes round every day to pick up the people who die in the streets. People tell horrible stories of new graves plundered and bodies carved up for food in the villages. Yet on the Boulevard, the down-at-the-heels central square of the place, people stroll about looking moderately well fed and well dressed. There is plenty of fruit in the fruitshops, and meat and cheese and wretched gritty black bread in the bazaars. The Russians have started a cinema and an Armenian theater, that flaunts gaudy posters opposite the Orthodox church.

It was there the Sayyid found a Persian who kept a shop. He was a Mussulman and told how the Armenians had massacred and driven out the majority of the Mohammedan inhabitants of Erivan. We bought a watermelon and ate it on the spot, while the Sayyid and the Persian chattered happily in *turki*. I heard the word *Americai* coupled with Ararat a couple of times, and asked the Sayyid what was being said—This man says that last year an American, an American journalist, went up to the top of Ararat and died there. He was poisoned by an Armenian. This man was his servant.

I was asking for details when several people came into the shop— He won't talk now, said the Sayyid mysteriously. We never heard the rest of the story.

Opposite the station a crumbling brown wall. In the shade of it lie men, children, a woman, bundles of rags that writhe feverishly. We ask someone what's the matter with them—Nothing, they are dying. A boy almost naked, his filthy skin livid green, staggers out of the station, a bit of bread in his hand, and lurches dizzily towards the wall. There he sinks down, too weak to raise it to his mouth. An old man with a stick in his hand hobbles slowly towards the boy. He has blood-filled eyes that look out through an indescribable mat of hair and beard. He stands over the boy a minute and then, propping himself up with his stick, grabs the bread, and scuttles off round the corner of the station. The boy makes a curious whining noise, but lies back silently without moving, his head resting on a stone. Above the wall, against the violet sky of afternoon, Ararat stands up white and cool and smooth like the vision of another world.

5. BAKH-NURASBIN

We got out of Erivan last night on a private and specially cleaned box-car, procured after long confabs with the station master and other officials and not a little crossing of palms. The Sayyid was superb, and used his Courrier Diplomatique style to great effect. When we were settled and waiting for the train to decide to leave, he gave me a great lecture on the theme of tell 'em nothing and treat 'em rough as a method of travel in Russia and the Orient generally. Promised to store up the pearls of his wisdom. Furthermore he attached to himself one of the men who swing lanterns, by name Ismail, a Muslim, who ran about fetching water and melons and even produced some rather withered cucumbers. We sent two boxes of sardines to the engineer and a package of tea to the conductor. Then, feeling our position on the train assured we closed our doors and opened our little square windows and got ready our usual meal of tea, cheese, bread and caviar, and after some hours' delay the train started.

This morning found us halted in a fertile but weedgrown valley between two ranges of bare pink hills. Behind us the two Ararats stood up tall in the gold shimmer of the dawn. Beside the track was a lean melonpatch that a skinny brown man in ragged Persian costume was trying desperately to protect from the inroads of the passengers on the train. We washed in an irrigation ditch and breakfasted hopefully, but it was noon and blisteringly hot before the train got under way. The Sayyid passed the time making great pan-Islamic speeches to little groups marshalled by the faithful Ismail, who collected round the door of the car and told of the atrocities of the Armenians and the sufferings of the Muslims. Meanwhile, out the other door I talked ragged French and raggeder English with an Armenian who told me the frightful things the Turks and Tatars had done. When the train eventually started it was only to run a couple of miles to this ruin of a town on the frontier of Armenia and Adjerbeidjan. And here we are, in an evil-smelling freightyard full of trains, beside a ruined station. As usual there is no house standing in the town. The Muslims say it was destroyed by the Armenians, and the Armenians that the Turks did the job. Every now and then Ismail comes to assure us that in two hours the train will start for Nakhtchevan and Djulfa, the frontier town of Persia that is our goal.

The Sayyid has gone to visit a woman who is sick in the next car. He comes back saying she has typhus, too far gone, nothing to do, will die in a couple of hours. We watch the other people in the car stealing away one by one. Then they bring her out and lay her on a little piece of red and yellow carpet beside the railroad track. She is a Russian. Her husband, a lean Mohammedan with a scraggly beard, sits beside her occasionally stroking her cheek with a furtive animal gesture. Her face is dead white, greenish, with a putrid contracted look about the mouth. She lies very still, her bare legs sticking awkwardly out from under a dress too short. Not even the red light of sunset gives any color to her skin. And the sun is sinking in crimson fury behind Ararat. From a triangular space between the slopes of the two mountains a great beam of yellow light shoots into the zenith. A man is standing beside the dying woman, awkwardly holding a glass of water in one hand. From the other end of the station comes the whining jig of a Georgian tune played on bagpipe and tomtom, to which soldiers are dancing. The woman's face seems to shrivel as you look at it. Behind Ararat a triangular patch of dazzle that rims with silver the inner edges of the two peaks is all that is left of the sun. On the wind comes a sour smell of filth and soldiers and garbage. The Sayyid, hunched dejectedly on the mysterious packing case in the middle of the boxcar, cries out feebly, shaking his head, Avec quelle difficulté.

Then without a word he gets up and closes the door on the side where the dead woman lies on the red and yellow mat beside the track.

Late that night, when I was wandering about in the moonlight with a glass of wine—the faithful Ismail had got us a bottle from the Lord knows where—trying to avoid the swarms of mosquitoes, I heard the Sayyid's voice raised in shrill discussion and often reiterated the phrase Courrier Diplomatique. Not being partial to discussions, I lengthened my walk up the track. When I returned everything was quiet. It appeared that certain people had tried to invade the sanctity of our private boxcar, but that in the middle of the discussion they had all been arrested for travelling without proper passes, which, according to the Sayyid, was an example of the direct action of Providence.

6. Nakhtchevan

Another freightyard, empty this time, except for a long hospital-train. Flies swarm in the stifling heat. The town is several miles away at the end of a scorching sandy road. The engine has disappeared and the few boxcars still remaining on the train seem abandoned. People lie about limply in the patch of shade under the cars. The cars themselves are like ovens. An occasional breath of wind stirs the upper branches of a skinny acacia on the platform beside the shed where tea used to be served out in the old days, but none of the breeze ever seems to reach the freight-yard. The Sayyid, sweating at every pore, is slicing a watermelon that we have to gobble hastily under handkerchiefs to keep the flies from getting ahead of us. Meanwhile the Sayyid delivers a lecture on the virtue and necessity of patience for those engaged in occupations cognate to that of courrier diplomatique. Having eaten all the melon possible, and having definitely discovered that we are due to stay in Nakhtchevan some eight hours more, I climb into the car and cover my head with a sheet against the flies with the faint hope that the heat will stupefy me into sleep. Baste it in the Dutch oven; the phrase somehow bobs up in my mind and the picture of a small boy watching fascinated the process of pouring gravy over the roast chicken, while it is placed against the front of the grate of the stove in a shiny tin onesided contraption. I wonder vaguely if I'm getting the rich sizzly brown the chickens used to get in their Dutch oven. Flies drone endlessly outside the sheet. Their droning resolves itself into the little song they sang in the Paris streets round the time of the signing of the so-called peace:

I' fallait pas, i' fallait pas, i' fallait pa-as y-aller.

Then from outside comes the voice of the Sayyid in his best style holding forth on pan-Islam and the resurrection of Persia. He must have found a Mussulman. One's head is like a soupkettle simmering on the back of the stove. Thoughts move slowly about in a thick gravy of stupor. Armenia. A second's glimpse of a war map with little flags, Russian, Turkish, British. What a fine game it is. The little flags move back and forth. Livelier than chess. Then the secret intelligence map. Such extraordinary cleverness. We'll exploit the religion of A to make him fight B, we'll buy up the big men of D so that they'll attack A in the rear, then when everybody's down we'll neatly carve up the map. The flies are droning: Carve dat turkey, carve him to de heart. Call the sections Armenians, Georgians, Assyrians, Turks, Kourds. But somehow when everybody's down they can't find the carving knife. So everybody just stays down and when they get tired of massacring each other they find they are starving. And death and the desert encroach, encroach. Where last year was a wheat field, this year is a patch of thistles, and next year not even thistles will grow there. And the peasants are beggars or bandits. And that's all there is of the map game in the East for the present. But the sheet's in a knot and lets in the flies. I'll climb down to see what the Sayyid's telling his audience.

The Sayyid is saying that the East must settle its own problems, that the Mohammedans of the world must wake from their stupor of acceptance, that they must drive out the foreigners who exploit them, and organize their nations themselves. He says many fine things, but he does not say how the little ragged children, tiny wide-eyed skeletons with hideous swollen bellies, shall be fed, or how the grain shall be bought for the autumn sowing.

There are a dozen of these little children, in all stages of starvation, crawling about under the cars looking for scraps; they are not like animals, because any other animal than man would have long since been dead. The Sayyid has talked to some of them in turki; some are of Muslim parents from Ervian; some are Christians from the Lake of Van; some don't know whether their parents were Christian or Muslim, and seem to remember nothing in all their hungry lives, but this freightyard and the scraps of food the soldiers throw to them—This is the eighth month, says the Sayyid. In three months, winter, and they will all die.

7. DJULFA (AUGUST 21, 1921)

That evening politik, as the Sayyid calls it, waxed furious. It came out that the engine could pull only two cars at a time up from Nakhtchevan to Djulfa. The contending parties were the Sayyid and a group of vaguely official Armenians. The station master was enticed into our car and fed tea and cigarettes and, when the doors had been closed to keep out prying eyes, was slipped a couple of paper Turkish pounds. Even then, the thing was not assured until, by a brilliant coup, a doctor, the most important member of the other party, was detached and offered a place in our car. The foiled looked daggers at us as we clanked out of the station behind a spluttering little engine. The moon was almost full. The track wound up through a craggy gorge beside a stream through cool intensely dry mountain air. I sat most of the night on the mysterious packing case beside the open door breathing in the cleanness of the sheer desert rock. Not a blade of grass, no life, no suffering anywhere, only cliffs and great escarped mountains and the stony riverbed, and beyond every upward turn of the valley crouched unimaginably new things, Persia.

And Adjerbeidjan that night slipped from out the shaggy present into the neat daintily colored past, as Armenia had the night we left Bakh-nurashin, and at another station of which I never knew the name, saw, while our nostrils were full of the stench of starving people asleep, and a pipe played sighingly somewhere teased our ears, the last glimmer in the moonlight of the tall disdainful peak of Ararat.

VI. OF PHAETONS

1. Garden of Epicurus

—The phaeton is ready, mssiou, said the longnosed waiter with a wave of the hand across the samovar. As he spoke the street outside filled suddenly with the jingling of bells.

When I suggested that the springs stuck into my back the Sayyid was offended in his national pride and sulked until on our way through the bazaar we upset a donkey loaded with clay pots that fell on a heap of watermelons and put everybody in a good humor. The phaeton was vaguely like a small victoria perched above a perilous system of ropes and wheels. It was driven by a stocky man in a white wool cap named Karim. In a little sling behind there crouched among some bags of oats an obscene broad-faced imp that Karim was continually shouting at under the name of Maa'mat. Thus with our legs stuck out over the baggage and our laps full of green and yellow melons and the springs of the seat cunningly gouging the marrow out of our spines we jingled, dragging a great bellying dustcloud like a comet's tail, past the Blue Mosque and out of Tabriz.

The entry into Persia had been made at Djulfa on the Araxes some days before. After the rawness of the death things and birth things of Russia, the balm of an old and feeble and graceful civilization was marvellously soothing. I remember scrambling off the locomotive that had brought us across the international bridge into the tremendous glare of sun of the valley of Djulfa where not a green tree grew among the pink and yellow cliffs that swayed like stage scenery in the heat that boxed it in on every side. Almost immediately we were ushered into a cool room with mud walls of a pinkish puttycolor on which were hung a couple of rugs, and little copper ewers of water were brought, and the Sayyid and I sat with our shoes off before an enormous and epoch-making watermelon being waited on by a tiny little man named Astulla Khan who had one side of his face swollen with toothache and his whole head bound about with a white cloth tied at the top so as to leave two long pointed ends the way people's faces used to be done up in the picturebooks of a hundred years ago. Then after lunch when mattresses had been brought and great pink cylindrical pillows, we lay drowsily through an endless afternoon, looking at the smooth mud ceiling and at the portrait of the Shah woven in one of the rugs on the wall, and out into the court where a tame partridge strutted about the edge of a little pool and where a kitten lay prone on a patch of blue and crimson rug in the sunlight. There was not a sound except for very occasionally the discreet bubbling of Astulla Khan's water-pipe from the next room. One felt endless ages of well-modulated indolence settling like fine silk cloths over one's restlessness. Perhaps this was the garden beyond pain and pleasure where Epicurus whiled away passionless days. At last the kitten got up, stretched each white leg in turn and strolled without haste over to the pool. The sunlight was already ruddy and cast long shadows. The hills beyond the Araxes were bright rose with purple and indigo shadows. The Sayyid got to his feet, dusted his trousers and muttered meditatively—Quel théâtre! Whereupon Astulla Khan appeared staggering under an enormous shining samovar and the business of the day was on again.

Out of the plain of Tabriz we climbed a dry pass and ate our own dust up a long incline until another valley full of poplartrees and mud-walled villages opened up at our feet and we found ourselves rattling and bouncing down hill again. At Basmich where we lunched there was a memorable garden. It was there the Sayyid first got lyrical. We sprawled under silvery aspens in a garden full of green grass and little shining watercourses and a boy with his hair cut a little below the ears like a pageboy out of the Middle Ages, wearing a tight belted tunic and straight loose pants of bright blue, brought us tea and a lapful of red apples. Then the Sayyid sat bolt upright and half closed his eyes and chanted in droning cadence the poem of Hafiz I have since found in Miss Bell:

> "A flower-tinted cheek, the flowery close
> Of the fair earth, these are enough for me—
> Enough that in the meadow wanes and grows
> The shadow of a graceful cypress tree.
> I am no lover of hypocrisy;
> Of all the treasures that the earth can boast
> A brimming cup of wine I prize the most—
> This is enough for me!"

—Quel théâtre! cried the Sayyid when he had finished and put a piece of sugar in his mouth and lay back with his hands spread in the soft grass.

2. THE SHAH'S WRESTLER

That night after a run through valleys sheening with poplars with a long range of eroded crimson mountains always to the left of us, we stopped in a dilapidated khan beside a very large beautifully built brick caravanserai, ruined now, of the type the road people always ascribe to the good Shah Abbas. The name of the place was Shibli and there we found a company of roadguards under the leadership of a mighty man of war, Hakim Sultan. Hakim Sultan was a stocky man wreathed in cartridge belts. He squatted in the most honorable corner of the room, pulling on a waterpipe, and looked out benignantly at us from small piglike eyes embedded in flesh. His hair and his drooping moustaches were dyed crimson with henna. Between prodigious suckings that made the water in the galian bubble like mad he told us that he had once wrestled before the Shah during Ramadan and had thrown all his opponents. With a rifle he was a dead shot. And Hakim Sultan's subordinates, fine lanky nomads a little less swathed in cartridge belts than their captain, who squatted about at a respectful distance, nodded confirmation like so many Chinese toys. Why, just five days ago in this very khan he had beaten off untold numbers of the Shahsivan. We were duly shown the bulletholes in the wall. It was admitted that the raiders had managed to make off with all the cattle in the place—But I drove them back into the hills. I sat and shot from this very place. One could imagine him squatting with his rifle, handling it as he handled his galian. Ah the Shahsivan, they were mighty men! Eleven of them had once disarmed a thousand Russian soldiers sent against them with artillery. They lived so far in the mountains a man who knew the road would have forgotten it by the time he reached their country. Their teacups and their youghourt bowls were of solid gold and they never counted the number of their camels. Such were the men, he, Hakim Sultan, spent his life in fighting.

At this point the oration was interrupted by the appearance of the host with a squawking chicken in each hand. Alternately they were presented to the Sayyid, who prodded and pinched them with a look of unearthly wisdom on his face. At last one was chosen and one rejected and the squawks brought to an abrupt end by the penknife of one of the nomads. Then, while from outside came hopeful sizzlings, the Sayyid took his turn. He described the countries of the earth from Berlin to Stamboul and their state and the condition of their politik, and how some were good and others bad and others, notably Turkey and the Bolsheviki, *tamaam,* finished.

Later he explained to me that he did not think either Turkey or the Bolsheviki *tamaam,* but that he wanted to counteract their propaganda—Diplo-o-omatik! he said, drawing out the word with the wave of an extended brown hand. When we had eaten bread and youghourt and cheese and chicken washed down with many tiny swagbellied glasses of tea, we rolled up in our blankets on the floor beside the window, through the unglazed lattice of which whistled the good keen air of mountain passes. I noticed the Sayyid sitting up after I had turned in, looking apprehensively back and forth between his moneybag he held in his hand and the prone form of Hakim Sultan. But we slept undisturbed in the Shibli pass.

3. POLITIK

Next day lunched at Shishmedosh, a famous place for hold-ups, a lonely khan of one room perched on the summit of a hill in the midst of a long desolate valley. More tales of the Shahsivan, of villages attacked and flocks and women driven off.

Night in a most beautiful village, Gareh Chaman, built on the flanks of a burnt-orange gorge on either side of a small sparkling river, full of trees and well defended by round watch towers. Carpets were spread for us on the roof of a house at the edge of the village under two enormous silver-trunked poplars; a samovar was brought, chickens produced for pinching, little ewers of water for washing, and the Sayyid, in his capacity of doctor, held a regular clinic, lancing boils and slitting ulcers and feeling pulses and distributing pills until suppertime. Then while we ate a lordly meal set out on chased pewter trays, the Sayyid delivered to the mollah and the owner of the village and the cook and the little boy who waited on us the usual allocution on the ingliz and the français and the americai and the osmanli in general and on the politik of Persia in particular, to the effect of Iran for the Iranis and beat the farangi at his own game. That night the wind rustled in the poplars and the stars sparkled with constantly shifting facets and in the distance jackals yelped.

On the road between Gareh Chaman and Tourkemanchai, where, by the way, was signed the first of Persia's disastrous European treaties, we caught up with the caravan of some of the grandees of Tabriz on the pilgrimage to the tomb of the Imaum Riza at Meshed. Such a prancing of white horses and a shouting of donkey drivers and a bouncing of panniers full of brighteyed children and ladies invisible under their cheddars! A fine whitebearded mollah with the blue turban of a Sayyid, descendant of the prophet, led the way on a well-groomed grey horse of which the tail and mane had been dyed with saffron. Not only the living but the dead were enjoying the benefits of the pilgrimage; at the end of the caravan came a long train of mules with coffins strapped to them on their way to reburial on sacred soil.

—If they worried as much about the living as they do about the dead, said the Sayyid, when we had got away from the dust and the shouting, Iran would be one of the finest countries in the world. If they would save the money they spend on pilgrimages and invest it in fabriks and railroads . . .

—But why factories and railroads . . .?

—Have you been in Germany?—Not for a long time?—Oh, but the commodité. . . . Everything is so convenient. Here things are done with such difficulty. Our peasants, if you knew how hard they worked, and nothing for it but to die of starvation when there is a famine in order that some grandee may make a fortune. . . .

Conversation was interrupted by the phaeton sticking firmly in the mud in the bottom of a gulch. We had to clamber out and Maa'mat had to be waked up and made to push behind and the horses had to be lashed and shouted at until at last the phaeton bounced, careening perilously, out of the mud and came to rest halfway up the rocky hillside. The opportunity was pronounced an excellent one for the eating of a melon, a long yellow one, milky inside with a flavor like almonds. It threw the Sayyid into a haze of rosy reminiscence, and when we had got settled in our pumpkin coach again, he started talking slowly:

—How well I remember when I first arrived in Leipsig from Constantinople. . . . Ah quelle commodité! It was so quiet at the hotel with thick carpets on the floors, and when you ordered anything, zut, it was brought! I dined there very well with wine, such good wine, and the waiter spoke French—I hadn't learnt German then—and was very amiable. When I had finished he asked me if there was anything more I should like. And I spoke my thoughts aloud and said without knowing it, Yes a mademoiselle. The waiter smiled and said he'd see what he could do, and I thought he was joking and went up to bed. When I was half undressed, who should appear but the waiter saying that the mademoiselle was waiting for me downstairs. I said send her up, but the waiter said that wouldn't do at all. And that is the whole difference between Oriental and European women. So I got dressed again and went down. I was so ignorant then of the ways of civilization; and the mademoiselle was very charming and took me to a cabaret where we drank champagne and there was music and she taught me many things. . . . Ah quelle commodité!

4. THE WHITE BEDBUGS OF MIANEJ

From Tourkemanchai on there was no appreciable road. The phaeton rattled over rocky hillsides, doubled itself up and leapt chasms like a flea, charged along the crests of ridges, dived into rocky defiles where at every instant we expected the whole contraption to do the trick of the one-horse shay. At a deserted caravanserai of the Shah Abbas sort, a roadguard, a most villainous-looking redheaded giant, met us and told us that last night a traveller had been sabred from the shoulder to the navel by robbers on that very spot. We gave him two krans and he went his way. The sun was hot like a lash in your face, we had eaten all our melons, and the water jar broke, and for all that day's farsachs we saw no living thing. Quel théâtre! cried the Sayyid at every lurch.

—Précautions. Toujours des précautions, was the burden of the Sayyid's cry as he superintended the cleaning of the roof in the caravanserai outside the gates of Mianej, a town famous for its flies, its gnats, its mosquitoes and especially its white bedbugs which breed a private fever of their own which has made the town's name renowned in the annals of medicine.

That afternoon we fought the flies and drank tea and discussed politik to the effect that Persia's policy should be to encourage European penetration from any countries that did not touch her borders, but to look with constant suspicion on her two great neighbors. That had been the reason for the pro-German tilt of the Democrats and Nationalists during the war—So far we have been saved by the fact that Britain and Russia can't agree. For a moment they did agree in the early part of the war and we went under, trampled like the grass of a battlefield. . . . But now they don't know us. They don't know what we will do next, and we don't tell our thoughts. Now is the moment to assure our independence. To do that we must have capital and foreign help, but not from our neighbors, from more disinterested countries. . . . But we must work slowly, cautiously, keeping our aims secret, toujours avec précautions, avec beaucoup de précautions. . . . As he spoke, the Sayyid wrinkled his face into an expression of almost superhuman cunning; then neatly catching a fly off his forehead, he said conclusively, Diplomatik!

The night was the first of Moharram, the month of mourning for Hussein, the great martyr of the Shiah faith. The mosquitoes and sandflies were so thick it was impossible to sleep. The Sayyid was oppressed by the fear of a lurking bedbug and lay in a small disinfected patch on the floor, moaning from time to time Quel théâtre! in the most dismal fashion. I covered my head and face with a bandana and walked up and down a little balcony smoking and watching good old Orion climb slowly into the sky. From the town came a roll of drums and in constant breathless rhythm cries of Hussein, Hassan, Hussein, Hassan. In the intervals dogs barked deafeningly. The air from the courtyard had a sodden putrid smell, and I could hear the bells of our horses jingling as they fought off the mosquitoes and continually came the sound of men moving in unison and shouting with all the hard-muscled ferocity of Islam, Hussein, Hassan, Hussein, Hassan.

5. The Humpless Camel of Djemalabad

In the morning Khouflankou, a jolly broadbacked pass crossed by a paved road built, I suppose, by the indefatigable Shah Abbas. Clear thyme-scented air to blow away the miasmas of Mianej. But the Sayyid refused to be comforted. He assured me with tears in his eyes that he had been bitten and would probably fall sick and die. Et après telle-ment de précautions, he ended sadly, as we breasted the last upward curve. Neither the scenery nor a new stock of melons nor seedless white grapes of ambrosial fragrance would distract him. He had diag-nosed himself as sick and it was due to his professional reputation to prove it, so sick he was; malaria, it turned out.

Discussed matters of religion at lunch in a rather mournful tone under an appletree in the ruined village of Djemalabad while a very old camel mangy and humpless looked at us fixedly with a "They'll come to a bad end" expression from the next field. The Sayyid said that all prophets had a little truth and that their followers should unite rather than squabble, since le Dieu was le Dieu by whatever name you called him. No, he was not a Baha'i, but he thought in many ways as the Baha'is thought, and they were good people, honest and tolerant and anxious for progress and education; he only wished there were more of them in Persia. But the poor people were very ignorant and fanatic and believed whatever the mollahs told them—Think, he said, suddenly sitting bolt upright,—I might have been a mollah instead of a doctor and a man of science. . . . My father was a mujtahid, a very holy man, and if the American missionaries had not talked to my father and induced him to send me abroad to study, I should certainly have worn a beard and a blue turban and became a mujtahid. Do you wonder I like the things of America?

Then the Sayyid got to talking with a very ragged man who sat a little way off from us and ate our melonrinds. It turned out that his father had owned this field and many more, but that the Russians had come and the Turks had come and they had destroyed the crops and burnt the house and killed his father, and now he was a beggar. He told the story cheerfully as part of the divine order of things. Islam is truly self-surrender.

6. THE ROBIN'S-EGG DOMES OF ZENDJAN

At Tarzikand the only place we could get to sleep was a contraption of planks perilously balanced over a cistern full of croaking frogs. The cistern was in a little walled garden of almondtrees. A terrific wind blew so that the coals would not stay in the samovar, and bits of the paper-thin bread at supper kept being carried away. As I lay on my back carefully balanced on the shaky planks the stars were like silver balls, Christmas-tree ornaments, hung on the swaying branches of the almondtrees.

During these days the Sayyid was silent, took quinine and watched his temperature. We spent another night at Yekendje, a glen full of huge poplars that grew along the pebbly riverbed like those silvery trees in Piero della Francesca's Baptism. There we took up our abode on the roof of the khan where was a little mud room into which retired the Sayyid and his malaria. We were waited on most charmingly there by a little boy named Kholam-Hussein who had run away from his home in Zendjan because, as he said, he did not like his father any more. When we asked him in the morning if there was anything we could do for him, he said that perhaps the Sayyid, who was a doctor, a hakim, could give him some medicine to make his complexion light, for he was very black.

In Zendjan the Sayyid perked up under the influence of a very aromatic drink named bidmesh, that had an odor a little like orange blossoms and slipped down one's gullet with a delicious drowsy smoothness. We made an attempt to dine in a restaurant in the bazaars but were told with brutal firmness Farangi nadjiss: A foreigner is unclean. The Sayyid could not even convince them that he himself was a good Mussulman and a descendant of the prophet, for he was wearing at the time a European felt hat. So we dined ignominiously at the inn and had a furious argument about industrialism. As we had walked through the bazaar, the Sayyid had made a great clamor about how hard the men who made copper kettles and the silver-smiths worked and how much better it would be to have it all done by machinery. He seemed to have the idea, universal in these parts, that machinery worked itself. I tried to tell him that the life of an indus-trial worker in Europe and America was not all beer and skittles, and even wondered whether those people hammering away at their cop-per pots, miserably underpaid as they were, might not get more out of life than, say, the steelworker in Germany, for all his moving pictures and bierhalle with which to amuse himself. But he snowed me under with a long list of famines and extortions of grandees and mujtahids and governors—No, he said at last, we must have fabriks and railways. Then we shall be a great nation.

The next morning we left the holy and dilapidated city of Zendjan. The sun glittered entrancingly on the dome of the mosque that was the color and shape of a robin's egg. The nadjiss business came up once more that afternoon. We were drinking tea in a little roadhouse when a hadji with a huge crimson-dyed beard who was sitting in the corner smoking a thick-stemmed pipe saw fit to object to our presence. But the Sayyid was on his mettle. He shot out a verse of Saadi's on the subject of courtesy to strangers, and without taking breath delivered himself of an enormous passage of the Koran from the chapter entitled The Cow. Then he stopped suddenly and challenged the hadji to go on from where he had left off. The hadji stuttered and stammered, but made no headway, and finally had to admit that the Sayyid was a good Mussulman and a learned man. He even handed him his pipe as a peace offering.

From then on the Sayyid's malaria was virtually cured. When we reached Kasvin he was chipper as a sparrow, and full of regretful reminiscences of the German mademoiselles—I shall marry a German, he said—I have a girl friend there who is a doctor, the daughter of a colonel. I think she will marry me when I am ready. I could not marry a Persian. They are very pretty but they are not developed. It would be like marrying an animal. . . . But all that will change; you will see!

7. The Guest Room at Kasvin

Kasvin was full of tall planetrees where perched enormous quantities of crows, that at dusk flapped cawing about the streets. We stayed with the Sayyid's brother and were royally wined and dined, although it was Moharram, in which month the Persians don't drink wine or allow any sort of amusement. There is something very pleasant about the simplicity with which middleclass Persians live. The rooms are often bare except for rugs and a few chairs and couches. There are no servants about; the sons of the house bring the pewter trays at meals and wait upon the guests. There are no beds or ornaments of any sort; at night and at siesta time mattresses and quilts are brought out of cupboards and unrolled. Everything seems to go on strangely quietly and without fuss. Out of the patterns of rugs and cups of tea and softvoiced subtle talk and the vaguely cloying taste of sweet drinks is woven an extraordinary harmony of indolence. In Persia—I suppose it's the same throughout Islam—life gives me the impression of having no surge and torrent to it. It is like a dry watercourse that has once been a swelling river, but is reduced to a few quiet pools that deflect the blue and the clouds, that within their limits perhaps contain more intensity of wriggling intricate life than ever the river did, but that are troublingly discontinuous, intermittent.

It seems to be the custom in Persia to turn in immediately after supper, and that night in Kasvin when I was left alone with my bedding in one of the upper rooms of the house, I was seized with an uncontrollable desire to walk about the streets. No use, for the house door was sure to be locked and I was afraid if I wandered out of my room I'd get into the women's apartments. As a substitute I managed to crawl through my tiny window on to a little roof from which I could see the flat roofs and the inky-shadowed courtyards of the town stretching away in every direction under the moon. Opposite me was the fat dome and the stumpy tiled minaret of the Friday Mosque. On many of the roofs one could see figures in blankets rolled up asleep; occasionally there was some movement in a courtyard. I thought of a story of de Maupassant's in which a girl stands up darkly naked in the moonlight on the flat roof of a house in Morocco. And for some reason a spasm of revolt against the romantic Morris Gest sort of Orient, and there's tons of it even in the East, came over me to the point of climbing in through the window again and filling up pages of my notebook about it. Admitting the spectacle, the crimson beards and the saffron beards and the huge turbans and the high-domed hats of felt and the rugs and the gaudily caparisoned white horses and the beautiful gestures of old men and the shrouded ghosts of women and the camels with their long soft strides and the dim richness of the lofty vaulted storerooms in bazaars, was not all this dead routine, a half-forgotten rite learned ages ago? It is in the West that blood flows hot and that the world is disorderly, romantic, that fantastic unexpected things happen. Here everything has been tried, experienced, worn out. Wishing myself at Broadway and Forty-second Street I lay down on my soft mattress. As soon as I was quiet I heard a drumbeat in the distance and voices throaty, taut, ferocious, shouting in quick alternate rhythm Hassan, Hussein, Hassan Hussein, as if it had been yesterday that Hussein, the gentle grandson of the prophet, had died thirsty at Kerbela.

In the morning before we left Kasvin the Sayyid performed an operation; then we jingled off in state, escorted by several officers of gendarmerie on their horses, leaving the victim bloody and groaning through his ether on a rickety table in the governor's dispensary. We ate grapes as the phaeton dragged with impressive slowness through dusty roads and the Sayyid talked about the revolt of Asia. First, he said, it was the collapse of Russia in the war with Japan that made Asia wonder whether it had been eternally ordained in the books of fate that her people should be slaves of Europe. Then the Turkish Constitution and the Persian Constitution had shown that the shady and dilapidated groves of the Orient had not been entirely withered under the killing blast of energy out of the west. And during the war, while Europe was fighting, Asia was thinking. Things moved very slowly in Asia, so slowly Europeans did not notice and said they moved not at all, but the time would come when the exploiting powers would suddenly find they did not know the road they were walking on. That was how things moved in Asia—Look at me, said the Sayyid shrilly,— when I was a small boy, I thought the Europeans a superior race, they seemed to have done so much five or six years ago; I thought the best thing that could happen to Persia was to be ruled by the British. But now. . . . I have seen all countries, I have heard all their propaganda, I have seen the money they gave in bribes, and their methods of fighting, all these highly civilized exalted races of Europe, and I know what I know. And what I know the muledrivers know, and the makers of clay pots and the men who rub you down in the baths and the farmers and the nomads. No, I will die gladly before my country is dominated by any European nation. And I am not the only one.

—As for the British here in Persia. . . . yes, I know they are a great people. I spent three days in London once; it rained all the time, but I went about and saw the people, and I knew then that they were braves gens. But here it is not so, not towards us, and for that reason I shall fight against them, avec diplomatik, as long as I live. And among the Turks it is the same, and among the Arabs it is the same, and among the Afghans it is the same. First we liked the British because they were better than the Russians, but now there is no pressure from Russia, and the British have changed. And there is not so much resignation in Islam as there used to be. Europe is teaching us, giving us weapons.

8. THE LITTLE PEOPLE IN PERSIA

Later as we drove before dawn on the last stage to Teheran, the Sayyid said again:—What is the mistake all the European powers make with regard to Persia? I will tell you. They think only of the great personages. They do not realize that there are little people, like me, doctors, mollahs, small merchants, and that even the peasants talk politik in the teahouses along the roadside. They know they can bribe and threaten the great personages and they think they have the country in the palm of their hands. But they cannot bribe us, the little people, because we are too many. If they buy me over or get me killed there will be hundreds of others who think just like me to take my place. What good will it do them?

It was just dawn; the sharp upward angle of Damavand, the great mountain that overlooks Teheran, was edged with a brittle band of gold. The wind had a sharpness almost of snowfields about it.

—And when you go back to your country, said the Sayyid,—do not forget to tell the Americans that there are little people in Asia.

VII. MOHARRAM

For Z. C. B.

1. DARVISH

Outside the gate where the dusty road winds off under the planetrees towards the hills sits an old man dressed in white with a blue turban. His beard is dense as if moulded out of silver. He sits motionless, staring straight ahead of him out of frowning hawkeyes. In one hand he holds up a curved sword, in the other hand resting in his lap he holds a book. The sword or the Koran. The horns of the swelling crescent drawing together on the world. People as they pass leave coppers on the corners of the prayer rug he sits on. The old man sits without moving, regardless of the swirling dust, squats beside the road on a piece of Manchester carpet with the face of an emir leading Islam into holy war.

In Persia there is a sort of holiness in the very fact of beggary. A beggar is an instrument by which a believer may lay up for himself treasures in heaven. In Mianej at the khan there was a merchant whose caravan had been plundered by bandits. He had a certificate from some mujtahid that Allah had bereft him of worldly goods and was sitting in the upper chamber patiently waiting for travellers to make him presents so that he might eventually start in business again. He had the face of a very happy man, of one who had stopped struggling against adverse currents. Not for nothing does Islam mean submission, self-abandonment.

And in every teahouse along the road you find merry fellows, ragged and footsore, men of all ages and conditions who have given up working and drift along the highroads, exploiting as best they can the holiness of poverty. They are certainly the happiest people in Persia. They have no worry about tax collectors or raids from the hilltribes or bandits in the passes. They go about starving and singing prayers, parched by the sun and wind, carrying epidemics and the word of God from the Gobi desert to the Euphrates. Tramps exist everywhere, but in what we can vaguely call the East, going on the bum is a religious act. All madness, all restlessness is from God. If a man loses his only child or his loved wife or suffers some other irreparable calamity he strips off his clothes and runs out-of-doors and lets his hair grow long and wanders over the world begging and praising God. A man becomes a dervish as in the Middle Ages in Europe he would have gone into a monastery.

I used to think deeply of all these things on my way back and forth to the telegraph station during those weeks in Teheran when my bag of silver krans had dwindled to a handful and my hotel bill grew and grew and every cable for money cost a week's board. It was in the early days of Moharram, the month of mourning, when there is no music or dancing, the month of the passion of Hosein, the son of Fatima, daughter of the Prophet. Every day Teheran was filling more and more with beggars and religion and hatred of foreigners. I used to wonder how it would be to sit under a planetree beside the road telling the story of the Shiah martyrs to a circle of villagers while people brought you tea and a bowl of rice with tears running down their faces at the tales of the sufferings of the great Imaum, son of Ali, whose flesh was infused with the substances of God, done to death by the falseness of the men of Kufa, dogs and sons of dogs, and by the wiles of Sheitan, the stoned one.

With the name of Allah for all baggage you could travel from the Great Wall of China to the Niger and be fairly sure of food and often of money, if only you were ready to touch your forehead in the dust five times a day, and put away self and the glamorous West.

And yet the West is conquering. Henry Ford's gospel of multiple production and interchangeable parts will win hearts that stood firm against Thales and Democritus, against Galileo and Faraday. There is no god strong enough to withstand the Universal Suburb.

Within our time the dervish, the symbol of mystery errant on the face of the world, will become a simple vagrant as he is in civilized countries.

2. The Teahouse

Hot afternoons the E.A. sat in a covered courtyard beside a fountain where goldfish swam, drinking glass after glass of tea and eating a curious cool jelly flavored with roses. There were few people in the teahouse: an occasional Armenian in European clothes, a Turk in fez and frock coat. In the month of mourning people stay in their houses. In a far corner the serving boys talked in low whispers. A fountain tinkled; there was the buzz of an occasional fly. The few sounds were flaws in the bright crystal silence.

Caught tight in the intent stillness of autumn afternoons, the E.A. used to wonder and puzzle on a continual jerky roundabout of ways and means. At the bottom of a vast still contentedness something miniature kept going round and round: how to get to Isfahan, how to get to Khorasan eastward, eastward to Kabul, to the Afghan mountains, to Canton, to Frisco. He pulled off ring after ring, but never the brass ring that carries the prize.

But what do I want to drag myself round the Orient for anyway? What do I care about these withered fragments of old orders, these dead religions, these ruins swarming with the maggots of history? Old men, toothless eunuchs asleep in the sun. It's in the West that life is, terrible, destroying sprouts of the new among the litter of Russian trainyards, out of the smell of burnt gasoline in Detroit garages. To hand Samarcand on a platter to that little Polish girl in the funicular at Tiflis.

As a sideshow it's still pretty fine, this vanishing East. The inexpressible soft, lithe swinging length of a two-humped camel's stride; the old men with crimson beards, the enormous turbans, white, blue, black, green, perched on shaved polls, boys with their hair curling troubadour-fashion from under their skullcaps, the hooded ghosts of women, the high-domed felt hats, the gaudy rags, the robes of parrot-green silk, trees the violent green of manganese spurting out of yellow hills, quick watercourses, white asses, the robin's-egg domes, the fields of white opium poppies.

If one were old enough and one's blood were cool enough there would be the delight of these quiet gardens of poplar-trees, the deferential bringing of the samovar, the subtle half smiles across the rim of tiny glasses of tea, the glint of scurrying water in the runnel in the center of the room, the bright calm of sunny changeless courts, the effortless life of submission to the Written.

But there are things worth trying first.

The E.A. gets to his feet dizzy with a sudden choked feeling of inaction and walks out into the broad street where the twilight flutters down like scraps of colored paper through the broad leaves of the planes. Hassan, Hosein. Hassan, Hosein. . . . To a sound of drums a procession is passing, gruff voices savagely passing, the warlike banners and standards of Islam, the hand of Fatima, the mare's tails, the crescent. It is the caravan of Hosein, sweet-bearded trusting old man, leaving Medina for Kufa on the last journey. There is no grief yet, but a sense of something circling overhead, wings of doom that plane above the dimming twilight, through the streets the drumbeat and the tramp of feet and the gruff cry of triumph, Hassan, Hosein.

After all are these gods so dead?

3. Malaria

The Russian engineer who said he owned a Ford looked at the thermometer and shook his head. Then he fetched his wife, who looked at the thermometer and shook her head. The room was full of people looking at thermometers and shaking their heads; a voice travelled from an immense distance and said: Nonsense, I feel fine. The bed was strangely soft, billowy, soaring above the heads of the Russian engineer who said he owned a Ford and his wife and the Hôtel de France and the cries beating out of brass throats, Hosein, Hassan.

There was a chasm. The City Without Bedbugs stood on the edge of the chasm. Insh'allah, said the Russian engineers, the city will not fall into the chasm, which is a hundred and five degrees deep. Then there arose a great prophet and he said, Ah mon ami, j'ai trouvé un poux. Avec le typhus qu'il a c'est très dangereux. Bismillah, cried the villagers. The city is going to fall into the chasm. Then spake the prophet: The City Without Bedbugs is doomed to slide into the gulf. Bismillah, cried the villagers. We must fill up the gulf or chasm. Whereupon they began throwing in their furniture and their possessions and their houses and their wives and children and lastly themselves. Intra venos, said the Sayyid rolling his eyes and shot in a tumblerful of quinine.

Then I was lying very long and cold and brittle on the stony tundra of my bed, and the Russian engineer who said he owned a Ford was explaining his plans to me in careful French. In a day or two the road would be open to Recht on the Caspian. Riza Khan was at this moment cleaning up the remnants of the Republic of Ghilan. Then we could drive the Ford to Recht, there load it with caviar that can be bought for nothing on the Caspian and drive back to Kasvin, Hamadan, Kermanshah and Baghdad, where the British would pay through the nose and buy by the grain what we had bought by the kilo. The only thing that stood between us and riches was a few hundred pounds capital to buy gasoline with. Now if I spent the sum I would eventually spend on the fare to Baghdad on gasoline and caviar, we would all get to Baghdad for nothing and have a substantial profit when we got there.

—But do you really own this voiture Ford?—Virtually. It's as good as mine.

Outside the wind howled and shrieked about the house. You couldn't see the courtyard for dust. Dust seeped into the room through every crevice. There was a half an inch coating of fine white dust on my pillow. The ramshackle building of the Hôtel de France shook and rattled as if it were coming down about our ears. At last the din grew so terrific that I couldn't hear the suave voice of the Russian engineer who said he owned a Ford.

There was a ripping crash and a shriek from somewhere in the hotel. The Russian engineer ran out and came back in a jiffy with his wife in his arms. Her hair hung snakily over her face and she was chirruping excitedly in Russian. The end of the roof over their room had blown off. It was a tin roof and waved in the wind with a sound like stage thunder. Surely the whole house would be down before night. I lay in the bed with the sheet over my nose to keep out the dust, and the sheet over my ears to keep out the noise, feeling very long and cold and weak and tired, and slid effortlessly into sleep like a trunk going down a chute.

4. Baha'i

The three American women were Baha'i Missionaries, one from New York, one from Chicago and the youngest one perhaps from some small town in the Dakotas. They all had the same eyes, spread, unblinking, with dilated pupils. We sat in a long dark room furnished in European Persian style, looking at each other constrainedly. The eldest women spoke of the persecutions of the followers of Baha'ullah in Persia, since the time of El Bab, the precursor, martyred in Tabriz: how they were not allowed to be buried, and how they could not meet, and how many of them held their faith in secret. She was old with tired grey hair puffed over her forehead and grey unfirm lips and a face full of small tired wrinkles. The Presbyterian missionaries who lived in the big mission at the other end of town would not speak to them because they were not Christians. They do not know that the service of our lord El Baha'ullah includes the service of Christ who was also a great prophet and the emanation of God.

Another of the women was a doctor. Her face was firm and thin and she was neatly dressed. She spoke of the sufferings of the women, of their flabby ignorance, their wilted lives in the candied gloom of the anderun, the sickness among them and the difficulty with which they had children.

The youngest one had come recently to Teheran. Her talk was full of miracles. She had come up from the coast in winter. They had told her it was death to attempt such a thing. Death has no power on the servant of everlasting light. She had crossed alone a great snowy pass that even the Kourds didn't dare pass in winter; when she came to a ford the swollen river would shrink within its banks; bandits had killed all the other travellers on the road but her; at every step she had felt the hand of God bearing her up, keeping her mule from stumbling, turning away the designs of wicked men.

It was dark when I left them. Outside, a procession was passing, first a few men dressed as Arabs on horses, then travellers on camels gaudily caparisoned, then men with heavy many-branched lamps of brass, then, behind a steel standard like a great flexed sword, weighted down at the tip by a brass tassel, flashing in the lamplight, penitents in fours beating their breasts in unison, tall dark men with bloodshot eyes, beating their breasts in unison to the agonized breathless cry Hosein, Hassan.

That was the thumping beat I had heard in the distance, that had made me restless sitting in the house listening to the missionaries talk of Baha'i gentleness and tolerance and fraternal love. From my room at the hotel where I sat reading an old and phony French translation of Euripides I could hear it still, sometimes from one direction, sometimes from another, shuddering through the dustladen air of the autumn night, the beating of the breasts of the mourners who followed the caravan of Hosein.

5. Hosein

Hosein, the son of Fatima and Ali, grandson of the Prophet, left Medina for Kufa, city of the first doctors of Islam, where his father, Ali, Lord of all the World, had been stabbed to death. Yezid was khalif in Syria and was plotting to poison Hosein as he had poisoned his lazy brother Hassan. The people of Kufa had invited him, the only surviving grandson of Mahomet, to be their khalif. On the first day of Moharram the small party of the imaum Hosein was met by Harro, who had been sent from Kufa by the khalif's officers to announce that Yezid was master of the city and that Hosein's adherent Muslim had been killed. Hosein was travelling with a few slaves and his sister and his wives and children. One of his wives was a Persian, daughter of the last Sassanid King. Harro, shameful of his errand, went back to

Kufa to beg that the imaum be allowed to return to Medina. Hosein's party travelled on slowly by night, for the weather was excessively hot. Hosein said: Men travel by night and the destinies travel towards them. This I know to be a message of death.

Arab-fashion they continued parleying back and forth until, the ninth, Hosein's caravan encamped at Kerbela, a little hillock beside the Euphrates. The army of Amr ben Saar surrounded them, under orders from Yezid to kill the men and bring the women to Damascus. At the last moment Harro and his men came into the camp to die with the holy ones. That night they corded their tents together and made a ditch full of fagots around them so that they could be attacked only from the front. Hosein bitterly regretted that he had brought the children and the women. They had no water.

In the morning Amr ben Saad attacked. Hosein's party was hopelessly outnumbered. At midday, tired from fighting, Hosein sat down for a moment beside his tent and took his baby son Abdullah into his lap. An arrow killed the child. Their thirst became unbearable. Ali Afgar and Ali Asgar, Hosein's two half-grown boys, tried to make a dash to the river to bring back water. They were killed. At last Hosein himself went down to the river. For a while the men of the khalif did not dare attack him, but as he was stooping to drink an arrow struck him in the mouth. Then the khalif's men rushed him from all sides. Thirty spears went through him and Amr rode his cavalry back and forth over the body until it was mashed into the mud of the riverbank. The head was sent to Damascus.

And on the last day Allah, about to hurl all mankind into hell, unmoved by the supplications of Mahomet and Isa ben Miriam and Moses and the two hundred and seventy thousand prophets, will remember the sufferings of Hosein, his agony of mind and the wailing of his women and the death of his sons and his thirst in the tents at Kerbela, and his eyes will fill with tears and whoever has wept for Hosein, whoever has bled for Hosein, whoever has suffered pain for Hosein will be saved, and will enter the gardens, the well-watered gardens where the houris eternally virgin wait under the trees eternally green.

In Teheran the tenth of Moharram dawns in terror and dismay.

All night the streets have been turbulent with torches and chanting and the hollow sound of bare breasts beaten in unison. In the early halflight the streets are full of watercarriers offering cups of water to passersby in memory of the terrible thirst they suffered in the tents at Kerbela. Now Hosein is receiving the first charge of the horsemen of Amr, the first flight of arrows.

In a big square in the bazaars the crowd is densest. On a roof chairs have been set for the diplomatic corps, Europeans in frock coats and uniforms, in white flannels and Palm Beach suits as if for a garden party, ladies in pastel-colored dresses, all guarded by a small contingent of Riza Khan's gendarmes. In every direction out of the covered alleys of the bazaars muffled drums and the gruff breathless shout Hassan, Hosein, Hassan, Hosein.

Officers of the cossacks and gendarmerie walking very slowly are passing with bowed heads, followed by led horses. Occasionally you can see tears running down a tobacco-colored cheek. Harness clinks, standards glisten in the sun, the hand of Fatima, the crescent with the mare's tail, green banners and orange banners, penitents in black tunics beating their bare breasts fill the square with a strange gruff hollow sound of pain. Then behind the device of huge steel blades weighted down at the tip by brass ornaments come men stripped to loincloths with skewers and daggers stuck into their flesh, spiked ornaments hung from their bare shoulders, men seemingly spitted by lances and arrows, sweating and dusty in the sun. Then after them, two long lines of men and boys in white shrouds belted with chains, each with his left hand holding the belt of the man ahead and with his right hand beating himself on his bare shaven head with the flat of a sword. The line moves forward slowly, swaying, groaning, beating in time. The blood runs down faces and necks and clots with dust on the white shrouds. There's a smell of blood and agonized sweat. From everywhere comes the gruff continual choking cry, Hosein, Hassan, Hassan, Hosein. The sun directly overhead flashes on the swords, on the swaying blades of the standards, festers in the blackening blood. Hassan, Hosein. Whoever weeps for Hosein, whoever bleeds for Hosein, whoever dies for Hosein. . . .

VIII. ON THE PILGRIM ROAD

I DARIUS KING OF KINGS begins the inscription on the great rock carvings at Bisitun. In the dimming afternoon light we could barely see the huge outlines of the figures. The great mountain rises to a peak at either end, each cut off sheer, making, the Kourds say, the silhouette of a house with a broken ridgepole. On the higher cliff, ochre-stained and rusty with lichen, you can make out the gigantic figures of bearded men. Archæologists hung in baskets from the top of the cliff can still read the bragging cuneiform inscription: I Darius King of Kings . . .

This road, from Hamadan that may have been Ecbatana to Kermanshah and the pass of Taqi Garra that is a vast stair leading down into Iraq, is one of those roads where have marched all the great parades of history. The rocks are worn and grooved by the shuffling of the feet of countless generations of men and animals. Everywhere people have scribbled on the rocks. A curious awe of history hangs over these valleys and cliffs, these stony riverbeds. In the echoing gorges the shouts of the Elamites and the soldiers of the Great King seem still to rumble in the distance among the cursing of the Tommies and hoofbeats of Russian cavalry.

In these last years History has revisited these regions in the shape of three devastating armies. The Turks and the Russians fought back and forth here all through the war. In 1918 the British pushed through here in their campaign for oil, building, or rather rebuilding the road as they went. The result is that there is hardly a khan or a village standing, that the desert, heir of the great parades of history, has nibbled away all the arable land, that in a day's run in a broken-down Ford you can't find a thing to eat except a bowl of sour milk, if you're lucky, in the tent of a migrating family of Kourds.

The road is full of pilgrims from Persia and all the Shiah world, for this is the good time for travelling; the rivers are dry, and there is no snow yet in the passes and it is beginning to be cool in the lowlands of Iraq. I can't imagine how they eat, particularly the merry and dust-stained families you see going it on foot, because the Armenian and I, for all our jingling of silver, count ourselves lucky if we scrape up one meal a day. These pilgrims are on their way to the Holy Cities of Iraq, Kazimain and Samarra and Nedjef and Kerbela, burial places of imaums, men who cast no shadows, whose souls are God's body. Rich people on horses and mules, women jolting in camel-litters, poor people on donkeys or on foot, caravans of small white coffins of the dead being taken for reburial in sacred earth. All day we pass them, splashing them where the road is muddy, giving them dust to eat, the Ford hopping and choking along like a dog on three legs, for the Armenian who drives talks English and wears a thinly disguised English officer's uniform and he feels as his the triumph of the Cross and the Allies over the turban and the Hun.

One night in the caravanserai of a ruined town I don't remember the name of, we had a little cell of which we had blocked the door with the car. The Armenian had left me there to guard the stuff and had gone off to scare up some food. I squatted on the low roof, ducking my head to keep from knocking down any of the fragile glittering glass balls the stars that hung down from the intense blueglass ceiling of the sky. The courtyard was full of little fires round which sat motionless figures of pilgrims; their talk was so low you could hear the munching of the mules and horses in the stalls. Occasionally a camel growled. In my face came a smell of dry sticks burning and from the kahwe under the gate a drowsiness of opium. Everything was spun of glass or ice; you hardly dared breathe in the intense fragility of the moment.

East and west and north and south were intense and bodiless presences like the being you used to imagine behind the windowcurtains when you were a kid. The four directions were torturing points spitting you through like the swords of Our Lady of Pain. Why is going east so different from going west; why is southward happy and northward miserable?

There was a whiff of singed meat in the air and the Armenian appeared below me with some skewers of kebab in his hand, a fold of bread and a white melon under his arm. We ate and fell fast asleep in our tracks.

Next morning the courtyard was empty. The pilgrims had all slipped away before light. We swallowed some tea and were off. This was the day we were going to drop four thousand feet over the great pass that leads into the Messpot. I felt itchy and depressed. Names of the cities I hadn't seen hummed like gnats round my ears: Kaboul, Herat, Khorasan, Isfahan, Shiraz. Baghdad would never make up for them. Besides it had a German sound, smacked of articles in the *Nation* on the Near East Question, of the Winter Garden. Oh, those pink Arabian nights.

> *And the ladies of the harem*
> *Knew exactly how to wear 'em*
> *In Oriental Baghdad long ago.*

After all, what was the use of going to a place that had established itself so definitely in Berlin and New York? Baghdad was in the locked-up plans of the German general staff, in Jake and Lee Shubert's storehouse, in the vaults of the Anglo-Persian. Why go messing round after it on the banks of the Tigris? After all, between the rivers they still showed strangers the wreck of the Garden of Eden and the actual figtree from which Adam and Eve pulled the leaves out of which they fashioned decency, morality and vice. That was something to look forward to.

Meanwhile the Ford was bowling along. We passed all the pilgrims who had spent the night in the caravanserai. The dry rolling plain was getting uneasy, breaking into gulches. Suddenly the plain began to flow through a gap in the hills. The road was drawn with it and we were going down a broadening, steepening valley. The valley narrowed to a gorge and we were zigzagging down the huge face of a mountain. Below us the hills dropped away in folds like enormous steps into a series of blue streaked horizontals. The Sea?—The Messpot, said the Armenian—Over there, Baghdad.

At Kasr Shirin everybody seemed to think I was in a great hurry. It was a pleasant pink and white town with porches held up on thin white-daubed columns. I wanted to wait and eat something, to sit around and see the town, but everyone seemed to think I would miss the train if I waited a second, so before I could help myself I was put in a vehicle with three gendarmes with rifles and packed off, as I thought towards Khanikin.

This vehicle was drawn by two mules and looked a little like the pictures of the ox-drawn beds of the Merovingian kings you used to get on little *bon point* cards they gave you when you knew your French lesson. It was the shape of a spring wagon—it had no springs—with a top and delicately looped side curtains. The woodwork was painted with pink and blue and purple flowers. In it the officer of gendarmerie and I lay at full length back to back, our heads elegantly resting in the palms of our hands, while the two men at arms squatted at our feet. The driver walked alongside and cursed at the mules.

So in reluctant and Shebalike splendor I was conveyed out of Kasr Shirin and out of Persia.

Across a crazy tumbled region of pink and violet and eroded orange hillocks, vermilion badlands, and the great pebbly bed of a river. Not a spear of green anywhere, nothing but this confusion of crumbling mineral color in the clangor of the afternoon sun. The vehicle plunged and lurched in the ruts of the fissured track; pink dust hung about us, and at last, shaken and thirsty and hungry and buffeted, we arrived at the railhead, a jumping-off place of jumping-off places. Yellow barrack sheds surrounded a patch of wheel-tracked dust where a few old men sat selling watermelons; beyond were some more sheds beside a track where stood three uncoupled freight cars. All this was penned off by fence after fence of barbed wire. This was the station and quarantine of the Iraq border.

The Persian gendarmes carried the hippo and escorted me gravely into the station building and then left me; the vehicle drove off and I was alone with the flies. After hours I found the babu stationmaster.

He was pompous and severe. The time was different from Persia, the money was different; this wasn't Khanikin; there was nowhere to get anything to eat. So I sat on the hippo in the shade outside the station door, trying to eat my watermelon before the flies did, getting stickier and stickier and dustier and dustier, and lonelier and lonelier. Down the track a vague squatting of "natives," characterless natives out of Kipling.

At last a wheezy black locomotive arrived, towing three grey cars with sunshutters, giving out from every crack the smell of steam and machine oil that brought all terminals back to my mind, the old Seventh Street Depot in Washington and the Grand Central and the South Station and the Gare St. Lazare and the Gare d'Orléans and the Gare de Lyon and the Estacion del Mediodia and the Bahnhof in Strasbourg. Oh, the meals eaten in station restaurants and the coffee and drinks at midnight in the little bars across the street! The oyster stew at the Grand Central and langoustes opposite the Gare St. Lazare, the bolted meals at Bobadilla and the chestnuts and churros at the end of the Calle Atocha, the pickled partridges and the snails washed down with manzanilla, all the last meals in all the terminal cities, meals mixed with the smell of steam and the thump hiss, thump-hiss, thumphiss of engines. Candy cigars cigarettes. . . . Have a nice chicken sandwich, individual brick of pure homemade Horton's icecream. . . . Nothing sold after the train leaves. . . . Oh, even the paper sandwiches and the smell of diapers on the New York, New Haven, & Hartford.

And all I could do was sit there in the dark amid screaming memories and stuff myself with watermelon, and watch, in the dim light of the single lamp on the station, the pilgrims from Persia who had lost, in crossing the magic line of British dominion, their merriment, their dignity of feature and gesture, the elegance of their rags and their tall felt hats, and had become as they crowded into the sweaty train mere featureless natives out of Kipling.

At last in great distress in the midriff from overmuch watermelon and alarmed by what a French doctor had told me, Monsieur en Iraq il ne faut pas abuser des pastèques, I curled up in the striped Tabriz blanket and went to sleep.

I woke up to find an Englishman offering a drink; the train was in

Khanikin; he had ridden down from some oil borings somewhere to the north. We sat up drinking in the dim light of the sleeping compartment talking about the Yezedis. All his workmen were Yezedis, devil-worshippers. He was trying to collect data about them, though it was very hard to find out anything very definite about them. The cult centered about a town or a tomb near Mosul, named Sheikh Aadi. They were supposed to be the last fragments of some Manichæan sect. They had a sacred book, but writing and reading were forbidden them. The name of Sheitan was holy and all the s and sh sounds were cut out of their language. They were supposed to have promiscuous love feasts on certain nights like those the Romans liked to ascribe to the early Christians. They always did the lowest possible kind of work, they were roadmenders and scavengers, and, a few of the richest of them, truck-gardeners. They were supposed to believe in the gnostic sevenfold emanation of God, but Sheitan they worshipped as lord of this world in the form of a golden peacock.

Eventually there was no more whisky and no more watermelon and no more about the Yezedis, and we went to sleep. When I woke up the Englishman had gone. The sun was rising over a vast plain dusty and treeless as a New York backyard that stretched an even battleship grey in every direction, without hills or houses or faintest hope of breakfast.

IX. BAGHDAD BAHNHOF

1. ANGELS ON WHEELS

You sit in a garden outside of the American Bar on Tigris bank under some scrawny palms. At the foot of the grey mud bank the Tigris runs almost the color of orangepeel in the evening light. At a fire of palm-stalks an Arab with his skirts girded up is frying Saratoga potatoes in a huge pan of boiling grease. As fast as he fries them he hands them out on plates to vague khakied Anglo-Saxons who sit limply drinking Japanese beer and talking about malaria, sandfly fever and dysentery. Round boats of wickerwork and skins (see Xenophon) navigate the swift river, spinning as they go. An occasional long wherry with a lantern in the bow shoots out from under the bridge of boats modelled on the one with which Cæsar crossed the Rhine. In the drinking of a glass of Japanese beer the day flares up yellow like a guttering lamp and goes out, leaving night, the scudding lanterns of the wherries, the arclights on the bridge and the dense Chaldæn sky embossed with stars.

From far away across the river come the hoot of a locomotive and the banging of shunted freightcars. The Baghdad Railway. The mazout-burning locomotives hoot derisively beyond the mud horizons. Oh, never-to-be-finished Baghdad Bahn that was to have joined the Sultan Shah Mulay Wilhelm Khan Pasha to his Eastern dominions, bogey of queasy-livered colonels in the Indian service, Moloch well fattened with young men's lives, phantom on lurid wheels that ran mad expresses through the eighteen-nineties up the steep years of the new century, only to smash up once and for all in the great bloody derailment of the War. Even now the apocalyptic vision of flaming wheels linking India with Constantinople, Vienna, Zurich, Berlin, Ostend, hovers over our heads like a greedy and avenging angel as we sit in the dark on Tigris bank drinking Japanese beer and eating Saratoga chips made by an Arab over a fire of palmstalks. Above our heads out of the dense sky the old gods of Chaldæa stare with set unblinking eyes at the river and the bridge of boats and the staffcars and the barracks and the littered trainyards and the fences of barbed wire and the trenches and the sodawater factories and the gutted bazaars and the moving-picture theaters and the great straggling stinking camps of refugees.

—Well, says the fat man from Illinois who is here to buy guts for the sausage factories of Chicago,—may be the Chicago of the Near East some day. . . . Still it'll take some booming before I invest in any real estate. . . .—Dunno, if I had a chance on some lots near the station, said the Armenian from St. Louis. . . .

There are no more Saratoga chips. We are tired of Japanese beer. Inside, cocktail time is beginning at the bar. I'm alone in the dark under the scrawny palms. From the distance comes the crazy hooting laughter of locomotives.

And Ezekiel too by the river Chebar in the midst of the great mud-flats saw angels on wheels:

Their appearance was like burning coals of fire and like the appearance of lamps . . . and the fire was bright and out of the fire went forth lightning. . . . The appearance of the wheels and their work was like the color of a beryl, and they four had one likeness: and their appearance and their work was as it were a wheel in the middle of a wheel.

As for their rings they were so high that they were dreadful, and their rings were full of eyes about them four.

And when the living creatures went the wheels went by them.

2. WATERS OF BABYLON

The Scotch engineer very kindly stopped the train for Kut to let me off at Babylon. In the grey plain the single track was two long flashes of sun. In every direction were gravelly hillocks of dust and potsherds that you could imagine to be the traces of walls, blocks of building, ziggaruts. This must have been about 125th Street. Jeremiah certainly had the right dope about Babylon:

And I shall dry up her sea and make her springs dry. And Babylon shall become heaps, a dwelling place for dragons, an astonishment and an hissing, without an inhabitant.

And Isaiah:

And Babylon the glory of kingdoms, the glory of the Chaldees' excellency shall be as when God overthrew Sodom and Gomorrah.
It shall never be inhabited, neither shall it be dwelt in from generation to generation; neither shall the Arabian pitch his tent there; neither shall the shepherds make their fold there:
But wild beasts of the desert shall lie there; and their houses shall be full of doleful creatures; and owls shall dwell there and satyrs shall dance there.
And the wild beasts of the islands shall cry in their desolate houses, and the dragons in their pleasant places. . . .
How hath the oppressor ceased, the golden city ceased.

—Morgen, said the leader of a ragged and dusty group of urchins who started to lead me into the downtown district—Bonjour . . . Babylon me know. . . . Bloody no good. The others kept up a chorus of Floos, meester, and danced round me with grimy palms upturned, undoubtedly the satyrs of Isaiah. So we proceeded to scramble over rubbishpiles for hours under the noon sun until at last we came, in the region of Times Square, to the Lion Gate and foundations of great paved halls that are supposed to be where Balthazar had his famous feast.

At last, dripping with sweat and with my mouth stopped with dust, I sank down under a palmtree in front of the still backwater that was once the main stream of the Euphrates, wondering at the peculiar effectiveness of the curses that Jeremiah had ordered the "quiet prince" Seraiah to write in a book and tie to a stone and cast into the Euphrates so that the luck of Babylon might sink as the stone sank. Jez I'd like a glass of beer, I muttered half aloud to myself. The urchins, their palms still outstretched, sat in a circle round me—Glas bier, cried the leader of the gang,—subito. And he ran off in the direction of the mud village among the palms.

A little later he came back with a bottle of Münchner Exportbier, cool and beaded, and some dates tied up in a pink bandana. That was one on Jeremiah all right. And it was no mirage. When I had finished that bottle the urchin said hopefully, Noch einmal, and ran off to fetch another. Revivified by Münchner, the hanging gardens began to shake themselves free of the dust. Bel and Mardruk sat once more in their starry chambers at the tops of their skyscraper temples. The sweet-voiced girls of Ishtar began to sing again among the palms. The song they sang was "Deutschland, Deutschland, über alles."

After all, if the mere hope of the Baghdad Bahn can make the dustheaps of Babylon flow with Münchner beer . . . But that certainly was one on the Hebrew prophets.

3. DECLARATION OF INDEPENDENCE

As in ancient Rome, dawn is the calling hour in Baghdad. Yawning, my guide led me through many lanes that still had the chill of night in them, through narrow crumbling arches, along passages between fissured mudwalls until we came to a flight of steep steps in the thickness of a wall. At the head of the steps I waited in a little dark chamber while the guide went ahead through a Turkish door of inlaid work. He came back in a moment and let me into an empty carpeted room— And the Sheikh Whatshisname? He patted the air with his hand— Shwaya . . . shwaya.

We sat down in the embrasure of a little window. Below, the Tigris flowed fast and brown, filmed with blue mist—Today, he went on, it is very dangerous for a patriot in Iraq.... We were glad to help the English fight the Turks. But now it is different. The English are like the old man of the sea: at first they are very light, but they get heavier and heavier. And if an important man is opposed to them ... shwi ... Cokus invites him to tea ... and tomorrow he wakes up on the way to Ceylon. This great man we go to see this morning is very much afraid to be invited to tea with Cokus.

At length a boy with a red kerchief on his head ushered us into a long plain hall with rugs on the floor and long cushions round the edges. After the required hesitancy and mamnouning we were settled against the wall at the far end near an old gentleman in dove-grey robes with a beautiful gold and silver beard; we drank coffee and eventually he began to address me through the guide. He spoke in a low warm voice with downcast eyes, occasionally bringing long brown fingers down his beard without touching it. When he paused for the guide to translate he looked hard at us and I noticed that his eyes were blue.

In America, he had heard, we had had a great Sheikh Washiton who had written a book declaring the independence of America from the Inglizi many years ago. Since then we had so far followed the precepts of the Prophet as to believe in one God only and to prohibit the drinking of wine. All this was very good. And now in the big European powderplay we had sent another great Sheikh, Meester Veelson, who had declared in the Fourteen Points at Baries that all nations were free, equal and independent. This was good, too. If such had not been the will of God he would have created one nation and not many.

The Arab nation, made up of believers dwelling in Baghdad and Damascus, had gladly helped the Inglizi and Fransawi to drive out the Osmanli who were oppressors and now were anxious to remain at peace and friendly with all the world, according to the words of Meester Veelson. But the Allies had not acted according to the words of Meester Veelson nor according to the principles of Sheikh Jurij Washiton. This was not good. Arab patriots had been driven out and imprisoned by the Fransawi in Damascus, and now the Inglizi, breaking their plighted word, were trying to make slaves of the people of Iraq. The Inglizi thought they could treat the Arabs of Baghdad and Busra and Damascus as they had treated the people of Hind. They would find that the Arabs were of stiffer stuff. They had tried to deceive them with mock kingdoms, when the lowest porter in the bazaars knew that Feisul and Abdullah, even the King of the Hedjaz himself for all his holding the holy cities, had no power outside of the guns of the Inglizi.

The Americai must tell his countrymen that the people of Iraq would continue to struggle for their freedom and for the principles announced by Sheikh Washiton and Meester Veelson. The last revolt had failed because it had been ill prepared. Next time . . . His voice rose ever so slightly.

When we got up to go he led us to the door. I asked my guide to ask about the plebiscite. The old man laughed. Oh yes, they had given out papers in the bazaars, but they were already printed with the vote for the mandate, so that the ignorant should vote for the government without knowing it. But only the Jews had voted and a few ignorant people; what man who knew his letters and the law would demean himself by voting anyway?

Oh, self-determination, where is thy sting?

4. Misadventures with a Consul

What with the mirage and the difficulty of following the road through the breaks in old watercourses the representative of the Screaming Eagle and myself arrived in Samarrah very late, after driving the Ford all afternoon over the naked pebbly plain of *the land the rivers have spoiled,* where you continually pass the mounds of crumbled cities and towers. It was almost dark when we crossed on the crazy ferry and saw in the distance the silhouette of the great ziggurat, like the tower of Babel in ancient illustrated bibles. Close on our heels came the Adviser in his high-powered car to find out what the devil we were up to. We all went to the house of the kaimakom, where we were given rooms freshly furnished in chintzy European style by Maple's. Dinner was a splendid affair. The climax of the evening came when the kaimakom, much exhilarated by ardent spirits (it is wine the Koran forbids) anointed all our heads with brilliantine. The representative of the Screaming Eagle was a very tall man who neither drank nor smoked. He sat bolt upright with an untasted glass of arrak in his hand and brilliantine running down his face while the kaimakom gave him a shampoo. The Adviser, who had brought his own whisky and had submitted cheerfully to the operation, leaned back in his chair as red as a turkeygobbler. It was a fine dinner.

It was on the way back to Baghdad the next afternoon that we definitely lost the way. When night came on our gas had run out. We were stalled in some tracks that might have been a road, somewhere between the Tigris and the Euphrates. After a great deal of palaver, for it was not supposed to be safe outside of the towns after nightfall, we left the representative of the Screaming Eagle eating a watermelon and went off in search of a fairly mythical village where we could perhaps find a can of gasoline.

Go, ye swift messengers, to a nation scattered and peeled, to a people terrible from their beginning hitherto: a nation meted out and trodden down, whose land the rivers have spoiled.

It's fantastic how this country is saturated with the Bible, how these desolate mudflats and rubbishheaps are scorched and seared by the cursing tongues of the Hebrew prophets.

Well, the consular servant, Abdullah, and I started out to look for a can of gas. He was a weazened brown worriedfaced man with a long crouching stride. We walked east away from the road towards some faint lights that might be a village. It was curious, walking over the pitted surface of the plain. There were stars, but they didn't seem to give any light. A cool dusty wind occasionally blew in our faces, a wind that smelled of nothing. Through vacancy from which shape and color and smell had withdrawn as a snail withdraws into its shell we walked and walked. Without speaking we walked and walked. Abdullah put his hand on my arm. We stopped dead. The ground dropped away under our feet. I remembered having seen some quarries or limepits somewhere on the ride up the day before. Through the gloom we made out a flicker of light. We smelled woodsmoke. Slipping and scrambling, we got down the incline into a muddy bottom of some sort, Abdullah walked ahead and I followed as best I could. We stopped before a burning kiln. The smoke eddied about us. Not finding anybody, we went on climbing up to the level of the plain again. We began to hear the barking of pariah dogs; as we drew nearer the village the dogs got our wind and came towards us, yelling in a pack. We made out some, mud huts and walked among them with the dogs yapping and snarling at our heels.

An old man stuck his head sleepily out of a door and showed us the track towards Kazimain. For a long while we followed the road until it disappeared and left us stumbling over the jagged surface of the plain again. This was discouraging. It may have been an hour before we found ourselves walking along a railroad track. Good old Baghdad Bahn! It might have been the Willimantic Air Line. Eventually we came to a station. It was dark, but a road led east again from it. The road went through a Sepoy bivouac. To pipe and muffled drum, soldiers were dancing among the high-flaring campfires. Kazimain, said Abdullah, putting one hand on my shoulder and stretching the other towards the horizon.

At Kazimain we made a knocking to wake the dead on the portals of the Persian Consulate. At length the Consul himself, in carpet slippers, backed up by his retainers with lamps, appeared in the door. He must have thought the perfidious Inglizi were coming to assassinate him. When he heard of the plight of his colleague of the Screaming Eagle he wrung his hands and ordered out his own limousine. We sped along the road to take help to the stranded consul and stopped only when the road ended at the edge of a deep pit. The Persian consul's chauffeur shook his head between his hands. He could go no farther. So the relief party started out on foot again, scrambling through gullies and ravines until, very tired, and each with a bidon of gas in one hand, we came again to the burning limekiln. At last we found the tracks of the Ford on a path. We shouted and yodeled. The yelling packs of dogs answered us from the horizons. Abdullah picked up a watermelon rind. The car had gone. Undoubtedly this was where it had been. Slowly, with a sense of gathering doom, he pieced together the whole melon. We strained our eyes to make it out in the starlight. Yes it had the markings of the melon the Consul Sahib had been eating when we left him. The car had gone, carried off by raiders, maybe. Abdullah squatted by the side of the road. He would wait there till the morning. I left him sitting beside the two bidons of gasoline and started to walk into Baghdad.

Walking along the dusty tracks, taking care to follow the ruts, is like walking through a dream you can't remember. The multitude of unfamiliar stars. The plain is terribly dark and empty in spite of the stars. The plain is crowded under its emptiness. Noise is shivering under the silence, ready to burst into the crazy yelling of pariah dogs. *Land shadowing with wings . . . a nation meted out and trodden down, whose land the rivers have spoiled.*

X. THE STONY DESERT OF DAMASCUS

—WHAT, YOU NEVER ATE A PRAIRIE OYSTER? cried the Major. Never—
Then you shall by heaven, before the evening's out. And so it happened
after we had given everybody airplane rides blindfolded on a board,
even to the cook and all the bearahs and one little man they dragged
in off the street, and while we were swallowing our prairie oysters and
taking a last nip of Scotch, rifle shots started snapping somewhere
towards the edge of town. Someone looked out of the window into the
rainy square and said,—Dear me, they seem to be firing. After I had
gone to bed above the lisp of rain trickling down mudwalls I could
hear an occasional shot shiver the cadence of the rain like a breaking
glass.

At breakfast over the bacon and eggs it transpired that a raid had
been made on the sarai, the government house, and that the safe had
been carried away—Never mind, I know who did it, said the Adviser;
he's a good friend of mine. I'll have him locked up before night. Those
damn native levies are probably in league with him. I'll settle him.
We had hardly finished our last cup of tea when a young man dressed
in a fine Persian aba of camel's hair, with an expensive pink agal so
heavily bound with gold thread that it would not stay straight but balanced ridiculously awry on his head, came stamping in with much
ceremony. He said he was the son of the naqib of Madina and a rela-
tive of Malik Feisul, and gave what was afterwards explained to me
to be an animated description of the heroic stand the caravan camp

93

had made against the raiders. He also said it was too wet for the camels to start and that we were to spend yet another day looking at the crumbled mudwalls and the date gardens of Romadi. Tomorrow if God willed. . . . Bukra insh'allah.

Then the Aviator and the Intelligence Man and myself were prevailed upon to visit the young man with the pink-gilt agal in his tent and I was made to ride out on a led horse with red tassels on the bridle. In the tent, that was an English tent bought in Baghdad, we sat on sheepskins and drank tea and ate Turkish paste and I fingered my list of Arabic words like a breviary. Bronzefaced people gradually seeped in, made polite ejaculations and were silent. Tallow smell of sheepskins. Flash of eyes, teeth, brown toes along the edges of a Persian rug and lean dry hands motionless among the folds of abas, and a rakish man with a black beard passing little swell-bottomed glasses of tea, that the young man with the pink-gilt agal, who turned out to be the Sayyid Mohamet, clogged with condensed milk with his own hands as an especial treat. Eventually we escaped to the open air again after a great deal of bowing and scraping on both sides and went back to chairs, whisky and soda and luncheon. In the afternoon the indefatigable Sayyid Mahomet reappeared and dragged me round to the coffee houses and cigarette shops of the small brick bazaar down towards the Euphrates. We squatted on cane benches, grinning at each other, speechless as apes, and watched the flies glinting in the sun above a muddy alley outside, and drank tiny cups of coffee black as night and perfumed with some herb or other, the herb of delay perhaps that induces the bittersweet drowse into which one falls waiting for steamers to coal and roads to dry and streams to become fordable and caravans to start. Tomorrow, insh'allah, if God willed, we would start for Damascus across the desert.

And what should appear, wheezing and popping through the ruts and puddles, but the rusty Ford that had brought me from Baghdad across the mudflats that lie between the rivers'? The Sayyid was immediately agog with it and after a great deal of discussion we set out through drizzly rain, lurching and clattering through puddles, spluttering down narrow lanes, frightening old women and chickens, making horses rear and break their halters. Half the population of the café had piled in, grave men in brown robes with beards like Micah and Ezekiel stood on the running-boards, little urchins hoisted up their gowns about their shoulders and ran after us, and every time the motor backfired everybody rolled up his eyes and cried, alham'd 'ullah, Praise be to God. At last when we had twice circumnavigated the walls and date gardens and the tumbled cemeteries of Romadi, the engine gave a final frantic explosion, there was a horrid buckling snarl from the differential, and the car stopped. The driver took off his tarboosh and wailed and everybody roared with laughter. Took the opportunity to slip back into Europe through a breach in the wall to the British officers' mess, where I sat reading the *Strand* until it was time for whiskys and sodas again.

After dinner and talk about irrigation schemes and uprisings I set out with two men with lanterns to find the caravan camp. A rainy wind was howling in our faces and continually blew out the lanterns, and we expected to find a raider in every patch of grey in the shrill blackness of the night. Eventually we heard a man singing and there came on the wind the growl and sharp smell of camels. The Britishers' servants left me in my tent in the care of an obsequious and soiled man named Fahad who set up my bed with great skill and bowed himself out. Then one Saleh, a crookednosed youth in an English army coat, came in and said with a fine cockney twang:—Me speak bloody English, messboy bloody English camp. Me boy take care seecamels. Then he stopped and with the greatest delicacy and good humor began to say it over again—Do we go tomorrow? I interrupted him. He rolled up his eyes, gargled an insh'allah and left me. I sat on my cot and looked about. The tent was crimson inside, with little decorations of hearts and diamonds on the flaps. It was round at the top, tapering to a single pole, and hexagonal at the bottom and gave me the feeling of being a worm in a fuchsia flower. Rain had come up and beat a gentle tattoo on the roof. I got undressed slowly, listening to the extraordinary bubbling and groaning of the camels. At last here was an end of colonies and whisky and soda and the *Strand* and canned goods and the American Bar on Tigris bank and the soldier-littered rail-scarred dumping grounds of the West. I wrapped myself in my striped Tabriz and blew out the candle. The rain beat harder on the sag of the tent over my head. People on guard round the camp called to each other at intervals with a long gruffening call. Once there were some shots far away. And just outside my tent someone was crooning a frail circular snatch of song over and over again. Something about Ali Asgar, Ali Afgar, dead at Kerbela. The word dead, Miut, I recognized because coming up from Baghdad we had passed the body of a Hindoo boy beside the road lying on its back with a stony smile, and Jassem had come back to the car from looking at it, had shaken his beard and said, Miut, and we had driven on. And listening to the song and the bubbling of the camels and the beat of the rain I went to sleep.

First Day: Woke up and crawled out of my tent to find everything else struck and everyone bustling and shouting at a tremendous rate. My delull (dromedary) that I'd been introduced to the day before and whose name I had thought to be Malek stood waiting, and her tasselled saddlebags they dragged the ground O! The datepalms in the gardens of Romandi stood kneedeep in mist that was just beginning to sop up gold in premonition of the sun. While I grasped the silver-encrusted pommels of the saddle everybody gathered round anxiously to see if I would fall off when Malek jerked to her feet. The hobble was loosed. Malek gave a grunt and opened herself like a jackknife. My head poked above the mist into the sunlight that stung red in my eyes. Then we turned round and followed the long string of baggage camels down the ruddy trail that led north and west towards Kubaissa, and for the first time I noticed round the shadows of my head and Malek's nodding head and Fahad's head the halo that so excited Cellini.

There's already excitement about safety money. It seems certain Bedawi of Toman are going to attack us if we don't come across with five pounds Turkish per head of cattle. We are being guarded by some fine hardboiled men on ponies, henchmen, if I got the name right, of one Abdul Aziz, head sheikh of the Delaim. From the moment we got out of gunshot of the sarai at Romadi we were on our own. During the afternoon I had lagged behind the main body of the caravan and was brewing tea with the Sayyid Mahomet and Hadji Mahomet, his cook, and a fauneyed brown youngster from Damascus named Saleh, over a fire of wormwood sticks, when there appeared suddenly over a pebbly hill to the west a bunch of men riding their camels hard. They stopped when they saw us and the wind brought us the groaning and gurgling of their beasts as they dismounted. The Sayyid grabbed his gun and began talking big, and the cook hastily packed the tea things, and we all rode hard after the caravan, saddlebags bouncing and rattling, dromedaries slobbering and snorting. Marvellous how not knowing the language takes away all sense of responsibility. I followed the rest without the vaguest idea of who was friend and who foe, calm in the recollection that my watch had gone by airplane mail. Of course it was a false alarm, but it made your blood tingle just the same. Almost as much as the air and the larks that rose singing from under the camels' feet and the uproar and shouting when a rabbit loped off into the thorny underbrush.

Second Day: We camped in a place called Sheib Mahomedi near a running stream. On the horizon to the north there are smudges of black smoke from the bitumen pits of Kubaissa. This morning I had to dress up in aba and ismak as Jassem made Saleh tell me that the sight of a European hat would make the caravan unpopular—English hat no bloody good. Arab hat good. So I am lying in all the pomp of a new Baghdad aba on a rug in front of my tent under a shining sky streaked like turquoise matrix. Beside my tent the big bales that load Jassem er Rawwaf's camels are piled in a semicircle round a fire about which all the gravest people of the caravan squat and drink coffee. Opposite is the English tent of the Sayyid Mahomet, which is where gilded youth seems to gather. The circle is completed by the bales of the six or seven other outfits that make up the caravan, arranged like Jassem's in a half-moon to windward of the fire. Besides the Sayyid and myself and the dancing girls on their way to Aleppo there is only a Damascus merchant effete enough to pitch a tent. Everyone else squats on rugs round the fires under the blue. The camels have been driven off to pasture on the dry shrubs of the hills round about the waterhole and stand dark in curious attitudes against the skyline. Occasionally you catch sight of a guard with his gun aslant his back, motionless, watching from the top of one of the tawny and steely violet hills that break away in every direction like a confusion of seawaves.

Down by the waterhole where I had been bathing I had a long talk in seven words and considerable pantomime with one of the Sayyid

Mahomet's retainers, a tall chap with very slender feet and hands, named Souleiman. He was asking about an Englishman named "Hilleby" with whose outfit he had been cameldriver in the Nejd. Hearing that I knew about "Hilleby" excited him enormously. He too dressed like an Arab and liked the sweet air of the desert—Air of desert sweet like honey. Baghdad air filth. Souleiman plucked a sprig of an aromatic plant and made me smell it, some sort of rosemary perhaps it was—Desert like that, he said; then he screwed up his face in a spasm of disgust—Ingliz Baghdad like that. "Hilleby" friend of Arab, not afraid of the desert, good. Then he took me by the hand and led me to the Sayyid's tent and sat me down in the seat of honor and brought me coffee and dates. After sitting there a long time trying to pick up a word here and there in the talk that seemed to be about the Nejd and how smoking was forbidden there and how great and goodly a person was ibn Saoud whom even the English called Sultan, Fahad my cameldriver appeared to tell me that my supper was ready. From him and Baghdad Saleh I got the impression that I was thought by the people of Jassem's outfit to be frequenting low company in sitting so much in the tent of the Sayyid Mahomet. Saleh said as much when he drove the camels home at sunset:—Sayyid he bloody no good. Social life in the desert seems to be as complicated as it is everywhere else.

So I sat alone in my tent eating rice and canned sausage, kosher sausage at that. I peered out through the half-closed flap—Fahad always had the idea I ought to eat in secret and used to shut me up carefully every time he went out—and tried to size up the other outfits in the caravan. Round Jassem er Rawwaf's campfire were my tent and the tent of the dancing girls, from which came a faint wailing of babies, and the little campfires of people with only a few camels who seemed to have attached themselves to Jassem's outfit. Then opposite was the Sayyid's khaki tent and the big tent of the merchant from Damascus and the two wattled litters in which squatted without ever moving a little Turkish merchant and his wife. At one end of the oval was the big encampment of the people who are driving the young camels over to sell in Syria, and at the other the outfit made remarkable by the presence of a fine old gentleman with a green turban and a beard like snow and a dark blue umbrella.

Blue smokespirals uncoil crisply from the campfires through the amethyst twilight. Camels stroll towards the camp in a densening herd, sniffing the air and nibbling at an occasional cluster of twigs, urged on by the long labial cry of the driver. The mollah is chanting the evening prayer. The men stand with bare feet in a long rank facing the southwest, make the prostrations slowly, out of unison. Gradually the camels fill the great oval place between the campfires, are hobbled and fold themselves up in rows, chewing and groaning. The stars impinge sharply like flaws in the luminous crystal-dark sky. My blankets smell of camel and are smoky from the fire. Once asleep, I am awakened by two shots that ring on the night like on a bell. There's a sound of voices and pebbles scuttling under naked feet. Saleh sticks his head in the tent and says proudly,—Haremi, bang, bang, imshi, go away. And I'm asleep again rocked like by waves by the soft fuzzy grumbling noise of five hundred camels.

Third Day: After a couple of hours' riding we saw palms in a shallow ravine and came upon the little desert port of Kubaissa huddled into its mudwalls among rocky ledges and sandhills. Was taken to see the Mudir and wasted most of the day in mamnouning, coffee, and civilities. In front of the city gate children were playing with a tame gazelle. Was carried off to his house by a fine fat sheikh and fed a wonderful meal of eggs and rice and fried dates and chicken. The fat sheikh is coming with us to terrify the bedawi by the augustness of his presence—All friends, he says, slapping himself on the chest. Was made to taste nine or ten different kinds of dates and not allowed to go to the bazaar, all sorts of attendants being sent to buy things I wanted instead. All this high society is rather trying. Eventually escaped with a book up a long rocky gulch to a deep basin in the hills full of mineral springs that steamed and bubbled out of potholes in yellow rocks. A very Sinai sort of a place. Jehovah used to come here in the old days.

Fourth Day: Great complication of social events. The Mudir came out to call on Jassem and the Americai, but was lured to the tent of the Sayyid Mahomet, who's a great little social climber, instead. Excitement and dark looks. Then apologies. Visit made all over again, interminable mamnouning. I squatted and grinned and nodded like a damned porcelain figure. Still the Sayyid carried off his infamy in fine style, spreading rugs and abas on the ground and then strewing on them with a grandiloquent gesture a basket of dates and a bag of Turkish paste that the Mudir distributed to his attendants and to the maimed and halt and blind who crowded round. A great day for the Sayyid. Bukra insh'allah, we are off.

Fifth Day: Malek has bushy eyelashes and eyebrows she can wiggle. Extraordinary how dainty camels are about their food. Some luscious-looking dry shrubs she won't touch and there are occasionally little rosettes with thistly leaves that make her eyes pop out of her head with greediness, that no amount of beating will drive her past.

Off first thing in the morning with considerable pomp, with the sun right in our backs and our shadows incredibly long, topped by crowns of bright rays. Rode with the fat sheikh, who kept producing legs of chicken out of his saddlebags. This is the order of our going: the outfits each start separately, with Jassem's usually first, and gradually fall into line along the trail; then as they get the sleep jounced out of them and the sun thaws their dromedaries the grandees of the caravan ride ahead. A couple of the Agail can usually be seen scouting far off among rocky hillocks on the horizon. At lunch the grandees squat about saucepans of rice and drink coffee and the caravan gets ahead and is caught up to during the afternoon.

This evening we're camping in a flat basin full of low aromatic plants, shiah and ruetha. Ruetha, that's probably the aromatic stuff Xenophon's always talking about in the Anabasis, seems to delight the camels beyond anything. Water must stand here in the rainy season. That rainy season, incidentally, must be about on us, for great showers are piling up to northward to everybody's delight, as they say a day's rain will mean plenty of food for camels. Also it keeps the Bedawi in their tents.

Sat in the tent of the Sayyid, in spite of Baghdad Saleh's remonstrances,—Sayyid he bloody loosewiler, whatever that meant,—and drank tea clogged with condensed milk I'd given the Sayyid in a moment of expansiveness, and listened to Souleiman, the man who went to the Nejd with "Hilleby," play wailingly on a tiny little lute.

Sixth Day: Enteuthen exelaunei a good bunch of parasangs with a general feeling of climbing up on a plateau. The trail, made up of many little paths padded soft by the feet of centuries of camels, wound around pinkish ledges here and there dotted with dry plants. In one place we passed the traditional skeletons. In a bottom we found the tracks of a Ford, the tracks of Leachman's car, they said. Leachman was shot during the revolt by the son of an old man he'd insulted. A delicious camping place at length at the edge of a basin where the dry shiah was tall as your waist. Three big rabbits broke cover as we were folding up our camels and everybody shouted and shot off guns in a most cheerful manner.

In the afternoon passed a small square stone tower.

Walked abroad after supper at the hour when they were bringing home the camels. A Bedawi whom I'd seen before riding on a white dromedary came up to me and said he was a friend of Malik Feisul's. We walked out into the desert together, he sniffing the air and saying that the air of the desert was sweet. His name was Nuwwaf. His tents were in El Garrá halfway over to Damascus. I taught him to say north, south, east and west, and he pronounced the words perfectly at once; while my pronunciation of the Arabic equivalents was so comical that he laughed until the tears filled his kohl-pencilled eyes. He took me to have coffee with the people who are bringing over the herd of young camels to sell in Syria. The Hadji, the old gentleman with the umbrella, was sitting at their campfire holding forth about something.

Back in my tent I found Baghdad Saleh and Jassem's little boy rolling me cigarettes. They tried to explain some terrible fate that had almost swooped down on the camels, but I couldn't gather anything definite except that it had been averted by Baghdad Saleh's single-handed prowess. It's very difficult to discover what Saleh means when he tries to speak English because, having worked in the Anglo-Indian camp in Baghdad, he has the deplorable notion that Hindustani and English are the same language.

It's the finest thing in the world to have no watch and no money and to feel no responsibility for events. Like being a dervish or a very small child.

Seventh Day: The mail plane passed overhead, flying high. Everybody looked at it scornfully without comment. Goddam cold and rain-squalls lashing in our faces. Everything more or less wet. Never have seen such exquisite distaste expressed by any animal as by Malek in the rain. Insh'allah the wind will go down with the sun. Sitting in chilly splendor in my gold-embroidered aba in my hearts and diamonds tent that lets in the wind most damnably for all its crimson lining. But who ever shivered in a broader wind?

The Sayyid's stock seems to be very low in the caravan. Souleiman had a fight with him about something, hit him in the face, so Baghdad Saleh says, climbed on his camel and made off for Baghdad. I shall miss the faint wail of his lute stealing through the bubbling, grumbling sound of camels across the camp at night.

Eighth Day: There never was invented a leisurelier, more soothing way of travel than this. The swaying of the camel is just enough to tire you out gradually, gently. You beat him just enough to keep your thoughts in a faint doze. You ride first with one person, then with another, looking back at the long trailing caravan like a kite's tail behind you; parts of it go out of sight in depressions, curve round hills. It's the way clouds travel, rivers flow. There are no orders given. Everyone knows what to do, as when birds migrate.

The sky is an immense sphere of clouded glass balanced on the bit of piecrust the earth; today it shines with occasional ruddy flaws of winter sunshine.

Towards evening, at the hour when your legs ache and your belly yaps like a dog with hunger, we came into a vast shallow valley running north and south. At the other rim of it was a row of long black things like beetles, the tents of the Delaim.

Ninth Day: Sweet wind and clear sky. A small party of Agail with a dozen or so baggage camels passed us coming from Aleppo. Very much like speaking a ship at sea.

We sat all day in our tents, O Israel.

Spent the day roaming about restlessly, trying to talk Arabic with Nuwwaf and reading Molière. There's some hitch. The fat sheikh from Kubaissa seems rather low. Much talk of a certain sheikh Mohamet Turki of the Kubain wanting an incredible amount of safety money.

Tenth Day: Still in the same place. Strange people keep filtering into camp, Delaim dressed in white, very large white-skinned men with waxed whiskers and their hair in pleats over their ears. They are friends of the Agail and the caravan is more or less under their protection.

From the first crack of dawn tremendous tumultuous speechifying went on at the campfire of Jassem er Rawwaf and has kept up all day; people jump to their feet and shout and wave their arms. The fat sheikh seems to be the general mediator. Jassem er Rawwaf is tall with prominent teeth and a beard slightly lopsided like the beard of Moses; he wears two head-cloths that fall amply over his shoulders, one white and one purple, and mostly sits silent directing the making of coffee with little movements of his long hands or strokes a string of amber beads. Once he got angry and leaned forward across the fire and said something slowly and deliberately that made everyone quiet down and nod his head. Later I asked him what the row was about. He smiled and shrugged his shoulders, at the same time rubbing his thumb and forefinger together with a gesture incredibly Semitic, and said gently, Floos, money.

All the desert seems to be prowling about greedily and appraisingly, waiting to pounce on our bales of Persian tobacco and the tempting herd of young camels.

Nuwwaf came and sat in my tent and talked a great deal about how the Ingliz were united and used their guns only to shoot strangers, while the Arabs were always squabbling among themselves and were very nice to strangers. At least so I understood. I agreed with him vigorously.

There's a great deal of polishing of guns going on.

Eleventh Day: Last night happened the first great rumpus.

I'd gone to my tent and closed myself in to read by candlelight when across the camp there began a great deal of shouting. Everybody started tripping over my tent ropes and rushing about. Baghdad Saleh rushed in to get his gun that he'd left there for safe keeping. Fahad appeared tremendously excited and kept shouting something equivalent to Man the boats. I stood in the door of the tent without being able to see anything, as it was very dark, but Fahad insisted I go in again, shaking his head in a most lugubrious manner. Meanwhile the candle had been knocked over, so I sat a minute in the dark on my cot, listening to the growing tumult outside. I had been plentifully nourished with horrors of Baghdad so I began to form pictures like the waxwork at Madam Toussaud's of Gordon at Khartoum. I thought of lithographs I'd had in my childhood of explorers in pith helmets being transfixed by assegais. The unfortunate death of the Prince Napoleon. Thank God I didn't have a pith helmet.

Finding that I was trembling and chilly, I went to the door of the tent again and lit a cigarette. Immediately a man I did not know ran by shouting something. I gave him the cigarette. He went off with it, seeming much encouraged. Then the Sayyid came up bareheaded and shaking and breathless, saying something about a gun. No, I didn't have a gun, but I gave him my cigarette. By the time I'd given away a handful of cigarettes the shouting had begun to recede in the distance. I kept wondering when the rifles would begin, not knowing how extremely careful with firearms the Arabs are. Then a great many people came and began to explain what had happened, all more or less unintelligibly. Did manage to gather, though, that the fight had started by one of ibn Kubain's men trying to steal the Sayyid's rifle. The rifle had been got back but there had been a fight and heads had been broken.

There were double sentries posted and everybody lay down heroically to sleep.

This morning we moved north across a thorny slope noisy with larks, to a camping place near a waterhole in front of the tents of the Delaim.

Went over with the fat sheikh to visit the Delaim. Their tents are very large, open on the lee side, divided in the middle by a curtain that screens off the women's part. To anyone born in a way of life given over to cult of Things they seem incredibly bare; a few rugs, some saddles and guns and a couple of piles of sheepskins, some cooking-bowls and the black ragged walls of their tents, are all the Delaim have to swaddle themselves in between the naked earth and the inconceivable sky. We squatted on rugs that were spread for us, coffee was brought, and I stared across the plain that stretched away indefinitely southward, where grazed great herds of sheep with men in brown robes walking among them like in illustrations to the Old Testament, while the fat sheikh talked gravely with the people we were the guests of. Then a woman brought a flat wooden dish that had in it a cake of unleavened bread, steaming hot, swimming with melted ewe's butter. Must be such butter that Jael brought forth in a lordly dish. A boy poured water over our hands from a little copper ewer, and the head of the house broke a piece out of the middle of the dish with a loud Alham'd'ullah. Then we stretched out our right hands and did eat.

In the afternoon went round and sat at people's fires and drank coffee and tried to find out how long we were expected to stay in the tents of the Delaim. Everybody said we'd go bukra insh'allah, but they said insh'allah so many times and rolled up their eyes so fearfully as they said it that it seemed pretty sure that the responsibility for leaving tomorrow was being foisted on Allah and that we'd stay where we were.

Twelfth Day: Terrific cold wind. Too cold to do anything but crouch over the fire with your eyes full of smoke.

Went to call on the Damascus merchants who brought me over the cakes the other day. Their little boy produced, to everyone's pride and delight, two or three phrases of excellent English. His elder brother knows about five words of French so we had a roaring conversation. Their father seemed extremely gloomy about our prospects and suggested that we'd probably turn back to Baghdad. But the little boy, who can't be more than ten, heartened everybody by saying,—We weel shoot Bedawi with the gun and keel him.

I don't entirely like the enthusiasm with which these Delaim people look over my possessions. Three superb rascals have just left my tent. They sat there a long time with baksheesh on the tip of their tongues. They felt of the canvas and of my aba and poked at the hippo and asked what was inside it, and their eyes sparkled with greed at the sight of the silver-incrusted saddle El Souadi lent me. I tried to glut them with cigarettes.

Bad. About noon. The wind's like a razor, and the camp is knocked flat with dismay. The merry men of ibn Kubain have called our bluff and driven off our camels from the grazing grounds. From the little hillock with the cairn I saw them disappearing behind the horizon. People rushed out from camp and shot off guns, but the Kubain people are stronger than we are, or at least they have more nerve.

Baghdad Saleh has just come in without his British army coat or his new red ismak, dragging his feet and looking very dejected:—Bloody Bedawi, bloody loosewilers steal bloody seecamels. He explained that he was asleep at the time or it would never have happened. He was beaten up and his gun was stolen and his coat and his new head-cloth—Bedawi no good.

I went and found Jassem, who was sitting in the lee of some bales of tobacco, beside the ashes of a fire. He smiled gloomily and nodding to the horizon made a gesture of coins running through his fingers and said with great emphasis, Floos, floos ketir, money, much money. So I went sulkily back to my tent. Well, the walking was probably excellent. It would be farewell to the hippo and its nonsensical contents. Perhaps we'd all be carried off into servitude in some lost oasis. So long as I don't lose my glasses, I was thinking. I lay shivering on the camp bed wrapped up in the Baghdad blanket. Molière had lost his flavor and drawing seemed a futile occupation. All the wind of heaven whistled round my legs. The tent was no more protection than a sieve. The leaden day was already shattered into tumultuous twilight when I heard a familiar delicious *cupalaoop* in the distance and the grumbling of camels. The camels were being driven home. They drifted one by one into camp, craning their necks absentmindedly from side to side until the whole space between the fires was full of their roaring and bubbling.

Thirteenth Day: It's all a farce played according to rules. The Delaim went after ibn Kubain's people and brought back the camels, and everything is where it started. We'll pay the safety money and I suppose the Delaim will get some of it for their trouble. The insh'allahs about leaving tomorrow are pretty feeble so I guess we'll round out the week in this accursed spot. My only amusement is sitting on the cairn and watching the flocks of the Delaim move slowly among the scrub-littered valleys round the waterholes. I'm sick of Molière. *And the stars in their courses fought against Sisera.*

Yesterday afternoon, after the crisis was over, the camp became very social. Groups of the Delaim and the Fede'an roamed about from campfire to campfire. I sat in state on my camp bed and everyone came and sat on the floor of my tent and was silent. Got very chummy with a young man of ibn Kubain's people who wore his hair in two little plaits neatly looped in front of his ears. He showed me his Turkish rifle and said he was the Osmanli's own man. Feeling it was up to me to do something to promote the Christmas spirit, I gave everybody cigarettes and handfuls of tobacco. The man with the little plaits I liked so much, I gave a box of matches. Whereupon he offered to go with me to Esch Scham or over the sea or anywhere. Then I would give him many gold pounds Turkish. I tried to explain that I was a fakir, a poor man, and had no floos of any sort, but he would not believe me. At that point Nuwwaf came in. Now Nuwwaf is a friend of Feisul's and a deadly enemy of the Fede'an and was much annoyed to find me so friendly with a mere bandit. I didn't have enough Arabic to explain to him that I liked these little brown hardboiled people better than the big white Delaim with their waxed moustaches, even if they were holding us up. He went off looking very hurt.

It's a cloudy stagnant day. The elders of Israel sit round Jassem's fire where Fahad is cooking disgustedly pots and pots of rice to feed this multitude. Now and then a gust of dispute rises and is caught up by other groups round other smoky fires, or there is an impressive clink of moneybags.

Fourteenth Day: Rained cats and dogs in the night, so we have to wait another day before starting, as camels are as helpless in mud as a giraffe on skates. That's five days going in two weeks. Damn all delays. I have the immortal itch to be gone from these cheezy hills where the sheep graze dully as maggots and the tents of the Delaim lie like dead beetles along the horizon. Was called on today, right after my lunch of oatmeal and condensed milk, by my Osmanli friend and the little crosseyed boy who is sheikh of the ibn Kubain crowd and a great mob of our yesterday's enemies. The little sheikh showed me with pride a German trench periscope he had; several of his men had field glasses. Everybody was having a social time when the fat sheikh and Jassem er Rawwaf came and drove them all away. Evidently the caravan does not approve of the way I get on with our enemies. That's the hell of being a hakim and sitting in a crimson tent. Everything you do has political significance. Nuwwaf came to see me later, looking very offended and making various unfriendly comments about the Fede'an.

I cheered him up by having Jassem's little boy bring us coffee, and then we walked up to the cairn and he pointed westward along the marked trail. Five days that way to El Garrá where his flocks were. If I could stay with him he'd have a sheep killed for me. I should stay with him many days, very many days, always; and for a moment, leaning against the enormous ceaseless wind that whined and rattled among the little stones of the cairn, I thought I would. To live always in a tent of black felt eating unleavened bread and ewe's butter, with the wind always sheer in your nostrils, moving south in winter, north in summer, for the grazing of the camels and sheep; to take a shrill-voiced Bedawi woman for a wife, to die of a rifleshot in a raid and be buried under a pile of stones beside the ashes of your fire and the round dungheaps of your last camping ground. Will the world hold anything to make up for the not living of that life?

I came back very hungry to my tent and had Fahad cook me my last can of kosher sausage. The tent soars like a balloon in the wind.

Fifteenth Day: Crawled out of my cocoon a couple of hours before dawn to find the stars crackling with cold. Everything had been struck. The camping ground was a struggling confusion of camels and drivers holding their necks to the ground while the packs were being fastened on their backs. The camels were struggling and groaning and roaring, the drivers were cursing and kicking. Jassem, always quiet, crouched over the last embers of the fire, warming his long hands. He was laughing quietly to himself when I sat beside him. He handed me a last drop of coffee in one of his thimble cups and then packed up the three pots and the cups and the pestle and mortar in his red saddlebags. Malek was brought by Fahad and nakhed; she lurched to her feet with such a jump that my head almost tangled in Orion, and we were off, everything at a jog trot due north towards the Dipper. A superb ride through the dawn across grass-sheening uplands to the great canyon of the Sheib Hauran, down round the face of red sandstone cliffs, Malek leaping like a mountain goat from rock to rock, to the water bed, where remained a few muddy pools from the last week's rain. There the camels were watered quickly and we were off again, scattering up the steep paths of the north side, I riding beside the old Hadji with the umbrella who rolled his eyes and cried Alham'd'ullah in the most groaning tones every time his camel took a leap. Then when we had scrambled up the last squared cliff of the canyon rim we were off under sparkling showers across the vastest, most pancake flat desert we have yet come to. Travelled eleven hours at top speed, and made camp in the dark, wolf-hungry and dog-tired. Wow!

Sixteenth Day: Reclining Roman fashion on my couch and looking out between the loopedup tentflaps at Fahad pottering very tired and cross among the cooking-pots from which steam rises silvery against a pistachio-green twilight. Up above the sky loosens into scrolled clouds of platinum and feathery purple. Barefoot Ali walks slowly across behind the fire, leading home a strayed camel. Ali, the most skillful of our camel drivers, is built like a beech-tree, never says anything, and walks with incredible majesty.

The journey was long and splendid. Gazelles were sighted. We rode through patches of scrub full of larks where now and then a rabbit broke cover under the camel's feet and sat watching a second with twitching nose before loping off into the blue ruetha again. White tablelands to the north that pinked to amethyst in the afternoon. And now the evening cry of *cupallyouawp, cupallyouawp* of the drivers calling the camels home from pasture.

After eight hours of the saddle my legs began to drop off.

It seems that the war in the Nejd is over. Ibn Saoud has captured Hael and ibn Raschid and all his wives and followers and is now supreme ruler of Central Arabia. There is a man in our caravan of the Shamar, a lean man with crazy eyes who gets to his feet beside his campfire after evening prayer every day and calls a challenge to any man who is enemy of his tribe to come out and fight. Every night his voice rises in a challenging cry that unfurls like a banner above the bustle and the camelnoises of the camp.

Seventeenth Day: Still headed a little west of north, wandering through gulches and between eroded tablelands. Camped about midafternoon near a waterhole in the dry bed of a sheib. To the south of us are high mesetas like those between Madrid and Toledo. Warm sunny afternoon. People retire modestly behind rocks to wash themselves and change their clothes. Wandered off over a hill and lay on a broad stone in the sun reading Martial. I have never been so happy.

In the evening sat beside Hassoon at Jassem's campfire for a long while watching the balled flames of ruetha, listening to talk I could not understand, and looking at the moon through the fragrant dark-green smoke. Drank endless little cups of coffee, the black unsweet-ened coffee of the desert, three times distilled, flavored with an herb that makes it bitter as quinine, as pervading as one of Wagner's great pilings up of the orchestra, as restful to the aching wind-rasped body as morning sleep. These people from the Nejd, Jassem and Hassoon and Ali, and the two little black men with the camel colts are the finest people in the world. Later I lay awake looking out at the moonlight, listening to the crunch, crunch of the camels' cud and the soft bub-bling of Fahad's waterpipe. If I had any sense I'd stay with Nuwwaf in El Garrá and never go any farther. Anyhow I don't care if it takes up a thousand years to get to Damascus.

Eighteenth Day: Nuwwaf and his friend went off today on their big white dromedaries. There had been discussion for several days as to whether the caravan should go through El Garrá or no. I suppose Nuwwaf wanted fat safety money in return for his protection. Anyway we are going northward still, probably to Aleppo instead of Damas-cus. They went off angry without eating bread. I might have gone with them. As I saw the two white specks growing smaller and smaller among the jagged folds of the hills I felt very bitter at my decision. It was during the noonday rest. I was eating rice out of the Sayyid's bowl with the Sayyid and Saleh, squatting in a patch of shiah. Our three hobbled camels stood above us, dripping green slavver from their mouths as they crunched and swallowed the succulent young growth of the shiah.

During the afternoon we veered more to the west into the teeth of a great wind cold as frozen razorblades. We are crossing a flat flint-strewn plain of a rusted purple color across which the camel tracks stretch straight and smooth like the path of a ship at sea. In the eve-ning entertained myself with a touch of that damned Teheran fever. Ate quinine in great quantity for supper.

Nineteenth Day: Chilly dawn; hoarfrost on the bare flints, fol-lowed by a warm delicious day riding sleepily through gorges and dry watercourses and over rolling flinty hills. Tremendous numbers of rabbits wherever there's a patch of vegetation, and pernickety-looking grey-crested birds; I wonder if they are hoopoes. The Hadji bit the dust this afternoon. One of those mules of Abdullah's that are always causing trouble bit his camel's tail and the camel gave a great leap and twisted himself in thirteen directions and off went saddle and Hadji and umbrella and a vast diversity of little packages and cookpots. The old gentleman lay groaning and crying Alham'd'ullah until everybody picked him up and cursed Abdullah and his mules, and the bent umbrella was straightened. Then he perked up and was set upon his beast again without seeming very much the worse.

When we made camp one of the camels that had gone hopelessly lame was killed. He seemed to know what was coming and stood tottering in the center of the camping ground, looking from side to side out of bulging eyes. Then one of the little black men from the Nejd, with his sleeves rolled up and his tunic girded high at the waist, jerked him off his feet and neatly cut his throat. Before the last twitches of life were out of the carcass it was skinned and, amid tremendous excitement and shouting, cut up. Fahad, all bloody up to the elbows, came back to our outfit staggering under the liver and several ribs. The liver was immediately grilled by being set among the embers, and the rest of the meat was stewed. I sat reading the elaborate idiocies of L'Amant Magnifique and made a noble supper at sundown off porridge and gobbets of camel meat fried with onions. Those onions are really the making of my larder. Went to sleep and dreamed of the sun-king and red heels tapping to the slow time of sarabands.

Twentieth Day: The sunrise was straight in our backs when we started out this morning, an unbelievable firework of grey and gamboge and salmon color; and so on sleepily swaying on Malek hour after hour, under a sky so intense that you seemed to see through the blue light of the world into the black of infinite space. Camped in the evening in a flat plain full of ruetha. Walked far out away from the caravan full of its noises of cookery and tent-pitching until a roll of the hills hid even the camels scattering to graze. There was no wind. The only sound was the occasional crunch or scuttle of a pebble under my feet. Suddenly I thought of the demons that Marco Polo tells about that dwell in deserts and whisper soft in travellers' ears, coaxing them away from their tents and their caravans over another and another hill, until they lose the north and wander in the waste until they die. It was almost dark. Condor clouds hovered thicker and thicker above the bleeding west. A little wind came up and hissed, whispered soft among the flints. My name, almost, hissed soft among the flints. Hoisting the skirts of my aba about my waist, I ran and ran until against the last twilight I could see the tents and piles of bales and the ring of fires and the confused long-necked crowd of camels being nakhed for the night.

Some people compute eight, others fifteen days to Esch Scham.

Twenty-first Day: There are two little conical mountains to the west. One of them I think is called Jebal Souab. The group of grandees riding far ahead of the caravan came suddenly across the crest of a low hill into view of a great herd of gazelles. For several minutes they did not see us. Everyone had a rifle ready. Then like surf breaking on a ledge the nearest gazelles jumped straight in the air and were off. In the click of a trigger the whole herd was out of sight. Hard luck, because my larder is quite exhausted and I'm living on rice and fried dates I get from Jassem. My cigarettes are all gone too, and the news seems to have got about the caravan because these fine people never let me stir abroad without smoking. People I've never been particularly chummy with appear with the makings on every side so that I have to smoke more than I want to keep up with their generosity. As for Hassoon, he seems to want me to smoke them two at a time. Funny sensation being hungry all the time. Am attended for hours by visions splendid of roast goose and canvasback duck and horsd'œuvre at the Bristol. When I wake up I find the air round my bed crowded with corn muffins and waffles. The descriptions of food in Mr. Martial's epigrams bring tears to my eyes.

Twenty-second Day: Splendid morning's ride through finest country ever, prairies of dry aromatic shrubs full of rabbits and strange white softly flying birds. Skirting the two little mountains, Souab and Damlough, under a sky piled high with rose and amber-glinting cumulus clouds, I was riding ahead with the grandees. Everyone seemed a little uneasy as one of the Agail had picked out a man on horseback watching the caravan from a shoulder of the mountain. Then all at once there was a cry of Haremi, bandits, and we all rode full tilt back to the caravan with clanky rattling of saddlebags and a waving of guns. Far away towards the mountain men on white ponies were loping down the hills like rabbits. Jassem rode up to his outfit and halted it in a little ravine. The camels groaning and roaring with their loads on them were nakhed and hobbled in a flash. The dancing girls tumbled squeaking out of their litter. The other sections of the caravan nakhed as they came up, until the camels were all sitting down squeezed together tight in an uneasy square. The pebbly bed of the ravine was full of shouts and squealing of women. The two horses were mounted, one by the Sayyid who annoyed everybody very much by stopping to put on his best aba for the occasion, the other by Abdullah; and the Agail and all the other combatant members of the caravan took up positions on the little hillocks round about. The Damascus merchant and his son took firm hold of me by either arm and sat me down between them in the deepest part of the gully, whether for their protection or mine I never made out. The little Turk's fat wife lay in a heap like soiled clothes at her husband's feet and now and then let out a long curdled shriek. Fahad pottered about scowling, tightening hobbles on camels, picking up things that had fallen out of saddlebags, muttering complaints as if this were all just another whim of Jassem's. Everybody sat hunched with expectation for a long while and I began to think again of the unfortunate death of the Prince Napoleon, but nothing happened. So I managed to get loose from my Damascus friends and climbed up on to the hillock above the ravine. There I found the Sayyid riding round and round like mad with his long sleeves floating behind him in the wind and his silver-encrusted gun flashing in the sun—Baruda Ketir Ketir. Guns many many, bandits many many, Bedawi on horseback many many, he shouted when he saw me. I replied that in Frankistan I had seen guns so big that the whole caravan could ride through one. That seemed to settle him for a while. The Agail were coming back from scouting about the hills. It was a fine sight to see them gird up their loins and tie up the long sleeves behind each other's backs. Jassem was quiet and smiling as ever. With one hand he held his gun, with the other he stroked his beard. The purple and the white headcloths fluttered behind him as he walked. There was a big body of men on horseback advancing towards us; nobody knew who they were. The Agail with extra cartridge belts scattered towards the hills again, and I joined the circle of the less timorous noncombatants who sat smoking on a little mound, presided over by the Hadji, who nursed in his lap his cherished umbrella and invoked Allah at every batting of an eyelash. We must have sat that way for an hour when suddenly a rifleshot and then another rattled in the hollows of the hills. Two men on white ponies appeared on the slope in front of us, riding licketysplit and occasionally shooting. A few bullets whirred over our heads. The group of the less timorous broke up in confusion. I have a distinct impression that the Hadji raised his umbrella. Somehow I found myself engaged in a long conversation with a Turkish camel driver. What language we talked I have no idea, as he knew no more Arabic than I did, but we managed to convey the most complicated ideas to one another while the Agail fell back towards the camels and more and more men on white ponies appeared on the hills from every direction, riding round and round us, shooting as they rode like the Indians in Custer's Last Stand that used to be the last number in Buffalo Bill's great show.

This Turk did not like the Arabs a bit, said they were a low and shifty lot. Neither did he like History nor the Germans nor Baghdad nor the British. He had been in the Turkish army during the war, had deserted, had three times been stripped naked and left for dead by the Bedawi. He had wandered to all sorts of inconceivable places, always trying to get home to some village near Brusa. Everywhere everybody had too many guns and there was no law.

All this went on for a long time, and nobody seemed much the worse for it, until at last Jassem stood on the mound and waved a long white sleeve in the direction of the attackers and everybody began to say that they were friends after all.

The raiders rode into camp on their lolloping ponies, gaunt men tanned black by the wind, riding in pairs, singing as they came. Their clothes were ragged and dirty, looped up with cartridge belts. Ibn Haremis is their name or the name of their sheikh and they belong to the Fede'an.

I sit shivering among my baggage in a cold wind that has just come up to spite us. Opposite me the Damascus merchants are dejectedly raising their tent. Tall desert people stalk haughtily through the camp. They have just made off with a rug belonging to the Damascus people who are setting up a great outcry. Fahad is cooking me supper, cursing under his breath. Jassem and Hassoon sit impassively by their fire grinding coffee. Their eyes shining under their headcloths follow every movement of their friends of ibn Haremis the way the eyes of a cornered cat will watch a dog.

Twenty-third Day: This is goddam tiresome. Here we are sitting on our tails again, discussing safety money. This ibn Haremis gang is a rare one. They've all been sitting in my tent looking at me and my blankets and the hippo, and numerous other things that people have brought to my tent for safekeeping. Such a set of walleyed, crooknosed, squinting, oneeyed, scarfaced cutthroats and slitpurses I have never seen. They go through all my possessions with gimlet eyes, and their hands feeling my blankets seem glued with greed to every fiber. I made a fatal error; they invited me to go see their sheikh and for some reason I was sore at them and refused. I don't know why, because I imagine they'd be very good fellows if you got to know them. May have unpleasant consequences, though. So I sulk in my tent with all the blankets wrapped about me and curse the wind and this blithering plateau and think of hot baths and steaks smothered in onions. Still it was worth it to hear their carolling song as they rode in pairs on white lolloping ponies into the conquered camp.

Twenty-fourth Day: Five camels and five pounds Turkish as ransom for the hippo was the khowa decided on, and now ibn Haremis is our friend and brother. Incidentally last night several old women appeared and sat round the fire and raised their voices in the discussion equally with the men. This morning the merry men saw us on our way. Great relief was manifested on all sides when our friends and brethren ceased to protect us and returned to their tents. During the day we kept crossing rocky wind-tortured ridges between flat patches of sandy desert. At sunset I thought I saw the mountains of Syria lying purple athwart the sun, but at dawn there was no sign of them.

Twenty-fifth Day: We were navigating splendidly this morning in the face of the perpetual westerly wind when some of Abdullah's ridiculous mules had to get lost in a tangle of dry watercourses. So we sat down beside a waterhole in a delicious sheltered valley, the Sheib War, with only half a day accomplished. Had the first wash in a week in a smooth sun-filled cave in the cliff where I lay a long time on the warm rock while my clothes were airing, reading Juvenal, to whom I don't kindle, notwithstanding his gorgeous turgid flow of indignant imagery. I smell rhetoric in him. Hope I left a few fleas behind in that rocky cave. It's terribly annoying to be cold and fleabitten at the same time. The mules are caught again and come with a great scampering and clattering up the canyon. Bukra insh'allah, we'll see the mountains of Syria and the Jebal Druse.

Twenty-sixth Day: Feel rather like the anonymous Wise Man who got there too late to offer myrrh or frankincense. Goddam cold and I don't care who knows it. Doubt if I was ever colder in my life. All day rode in a bitter wind under a bright sky over terrific uplands of sharp glinting flints. About the first real continuous desert; no trace of vegetation. All our fires are of dry camel dung, jelle, collected from an old camping place we passed. Here we are camped under a cairn at the head of Wadi Mia which is diversely said to be four and eight days from Damascus. Shiver and pray for supper. Fleas.

Twenty-seventh Day: Have a sort of suspicion that this is Christmas Day, but as I'm not quite sure what the date was when I left Baghdad, I may have calculated wrong. Ate kastowi for lunch, rice with my last onions for supper. Cold as blazes. Long desolate ride over purple hills strewn with sharp flints into a wind colder and sharper than all the flints from here to Jericho. This must be the highest part of the hog-back, as there comes in the rain an occasional spit of sleet. Put my foot in it terribly this evening. Was taking my habitual before-supper stroll to the highest hill round about the camp, and had paused on the crest to look down through grey smudges of mist into the vast putty-colored wilderness ahead of us. In front of me, standing out against the last silvery light like monsters of an eocene world, two camels were making love, twining their snaky necks together with flopping slob-bering lips and groanings through yellow teeth. Clumsily, sensitively under the aluminum twilight the act was accomplished. I had climbed on a rock to see further, when I saw Jassem running up the slope with his fieldglasses in his hand, hallooing desperately. I went down to him and found him wild. All day the caravan had been manoeuvring to keep out of sight of some black tents pitched in the next valley and there I was standing like a monument on top of the hill, visible for a day's journey in every direction. He vented his wrath, and I my shame, by throwing stones at the camels and driving them back to camp.

Twenty-eighth Day: Bitter rain in misty squalls. A North Sea day with nary a glimpse of sun. Rode from before dawn till after dark through howling flinty wilderness. The Agail laugh at me at night sitting round the fire because the stinging smoke of jelle makes my eyes water. Hassoon can hold his face almost to the flame in the thickest of the smoke without a flicker of his eyelids. Held high discourse about America. It seems that some of the Agail have been there and come back with the word that it was a land full of floos. The coffee we were drinking came from Santos, so everybody thought I lived where the coffee came from. Everyone wondered at the great iron ships going over the sea; and sitting there in the desert round the glowing fire of cameldung under a night of unfathomable misty blackness, we felt the suction of the great machine, the glint of whirring nickel, the shine of celluloid and enamel, the crackle of banknotes fingered in banks, the click and grinding of oiled wheels. I made a great speech and said that if I had any sense I would live in the desert with the Agail and never go back; but they took it as a compliment and did not understand. Jassem asked me, then, what kind of a hakim I was in my country, a great man like Cokus? No not quite.

The Hadji has no luck. He slept in my tent last night as it was very wet outside, and naturally the tent had to blow down and half the camels to stampede, so that the poor old gentleman was forgotten and trampled on and finally picked prone and groaning from under the collapsed bed. And the umbrella underwent further injuries.

My shoes are split and I have chilblains.

Twenty-ninth Day: Stuck again. Fifteen camels lame from the heavy going of the last few days. Shivered in wet tents all day. Sat all afternoon in the tent of the Sayyid, while his cook Hadji Mahomet told stories. I could not follow them at all, but they began with such pomaded suaveness of Once upon a time there lived . . . and worked up to such pitch of excitement where everybody cried Ei Wallah and Allah and wallowed in such smutty chortlings when all hands wriggled in their places and curled up their brown toes with delight that it was almost as if I had understood the words. Then the Damascus merchant's little boy sang and everybody ate dates and drank tea. Between the verses of love-songs everyone cries Allah and groans in a most melancholy manner.

Thirtieth Day: Began in mist and despair. Then phantom hills to the west seemed to promise Syria and its fleshpots, and the sun came out and the immense disk of purple flint shone like a shattered mirror.

Thirty-first Day: Splendid frosty morning. Interminably westward across this petrified sea of flints. Continually hungry. Hours before noon I start thinking of the taste of kastowi, a delicious molasses-brown concoction of ewe's butter and dates fried up together, and in the evening I massacre the rice and bread almost without tasting it. Last night I dreamed of dining at the Bristol in Marseilles, of eating the crackly brown skin of roast goose. It makes me feel terribly soft. No one else seems to mind half rations. The Arabs are the most frugal people I ever consorted with.

Thirty-second Day: Half day on. Camels low, as there has been no food for several days. Let 'em take a thousand years to get to Damascus. I don't care. I'll never sit about such fragrant fires again, or with such fine people. Christ, I feel well, bearded, fullblooded, all the bile out of my belly, all the wrinkles ironed out of my mind by the great cold purple flinty flatiron of the desert.

The Sayyid and Damascus Saleh have had a row, I don't know what about.

Thirty-third Day: A new wind has come up, Hawa Esch Scham, the wind of Damascus, they call it. Everything is pink and warm colored like the ears of a jackrabbit seen for a second against the sun. We have made a splendid camp on a shiah-covered slope. At the end of a trough to the northwest are tall promontory hills jutting into the desert, the actual hills of Syria. Beyond them is Tidmor that I am not fated to see—Alas, Zenobia. Shoes split, feet chilblained, hands stiff with cold, but jolly as a lark. Wish I had a rum punch, hot, with a slice of lemon and two cloves.

Thirty-fourth Day: Through rocky defiles and over patches of sandy desert with the hills of Syria gathering like a herd of cattle to the west. This afternoon we were almost held up again. Two of the Agail sighted guns and headcloths at the opening of a deep ravine the trail leads through, so in a jiffy the caravan did a right-about-face, and went off to the south, while the grandees on their dromedaries rode on towards the ambuscade with their guns cocked. These people wore various-colored headcloths and were from the Jebal Druse. I don't think they were actually Druses, but rabble from the outskirts, half Bedawi and half Druse. They asked to see the mad Frank who was wandering about the desert, and upon my being produced looked at me critically but amiably. A lot of big talk followed. They were finally bought off with fifteen pounds Turkish and a sack of dates. I don't think they could have done us much mischief anyway as few of them were mounted.

Thirty-fifth Day: We are riding between two ranges of barren mountains, pink and ochre and purple and indigo in the shadows, reflected in long streaks of stagnant water that leaves where it dries the sand cracked and mottled like alligator hide. Now that we are out of danger from the Bedawi everybody is worried about the French camel corps, as there is a duty on tobacco and camels and the game is to smuggle through. How a caravan of five hundred camels can slip into Damascus unnoticed is beyond me, but one should never deny wonders. Everybody is restless and excited like the last day out on an ocean liner.

Thirty-sixth Day: All things have come to pass. We are camped over against Dmair, huddled in a little hollow of the hills. We are in Syria. Blue smoke goes up from the village and is lost in the blue of the ridges in front of Lebanon. Further south the Jebal Sheikh sits hunched and hoary. There are goats and flocks of sheep grazing round about the camp. I'd like to go to Dmair, but Jassem won't let me for fear of waking the drowsy customs officers. Various inhabitants of Dmair are coming out to us on camels and donkeys, however. I almost wish we were still out in the desert, leaving instead of arriving, but oh, for a hot bath and food, food, food.

Thirty-seventh Day: O those Sayyids. The unforgettable entry into Damascus.

Last night the caravan camp was full of goings and comings, deep talk round Jassem's fire, and groaning and bubbling of camels. The last thing I heard as I went to sleep was the clink of money, gold pounds Turkish being counted from palm into palm. In the morning when I woke up the camp looked as if a cyclone had struck it. Half the camels, most of the bales of tobacco and rugs and, I imagine, opium had vanished in blue haze. Jassem sat quietly grinding his coffee, occasionally stroking his black beard. As I was drinking coffee with him he gently insinuated the thought that when I talked with the French in Damascus I should not know how many camels nor how we had come. I told him I had a bad head for figures.

Then Abdullah's white stallion was brought up and I perched my galled posterior on an execrable saddle and we were off towards Damascus, I on my stallion, the Sayyid on his dromedary, the Sayyid's cook on a skittish white camel, and one of the Agail on foot to put us on the road. That morning seemed endless. We kept losing the road, first over shaggy uplands and then in a fat valley full of pasture lands, patches of green sesame and alfalfa, apple orchards, pink adobe houses. Eventually the Sayyid took pity on my agonized bouncing on the stirrupless stallion and let me ride his dromedary. The white camel did not like the smell of civilization and kept trying to bolt back to the desert. At last, deliriously hungry, galled, limping, tired to a frazzle, we got to a village where we left our beasts in the inn, ate all too frugally of beans and cheese and kebab, and then drove, lolling like Zeus in his chariot of eagles, in a landau into Damascus. Then before I could put food to my mouth or water to my skin I had to go to see all the Sayyid's relatives, old men with beards in the Scribes' bazaar, people in mysterious courtyards who were adherents of Feisul's and plotting against the French, a tailor in a tailor shop, the keeper of a café frequented by the Agail; with all these, interminable scraping and mamnouning, until at last we found ourselves in contact with the forces of civilization. We had left the cab outside a café where we were palavering busily, I too dazed with hunger and unwashedness to know what was going on; on coming out we found a drunken French officer sitting in it. The Sayyid protested that it was our cab and the Frenchman started spouting abuse, and the Sayyid drew his little dagger and there would have been the devil to pay if the Frenchman had not hazily realized that I was talking French to him. He immediately apologized profusely and embraced the Sayyid in the name of the Allies and we all rode off together singing "la Madelon de la Victoire" to a most Parisian gin-mill in the main square. The Sayyid sat outside while we Occidentals went in and drank I don't know how many glasses of absinthe in the name of Liberty, Fraternity and Equality. In a pink indeterminate and vaguely swishing cloud I drove to the hotel, somehow got rid of the Frenchman and the Sayyid, and at last was alone sprawling buoyant in a warm bath that tasted of absinthe, smelled of absinthe, swished and simmered drowsily, tingled pinkly with absinthe.

XI. TABLE D'HOTE

1. The wind blows up the tent like a balloon.
   The tent plunges tugging at pegged ropes,
   about to wrench loose and soar
   above wormwood-carpeted canyons
   and flinty sawtooth hills,
   up into the driven night
   and the howling clouds.
   Tight
   as a worm curls wickedly
   round the stamen of a fuchsia,
   a man curls his hands round a candle.
   The flame totters in the wind,
   flares to lick his hands,
   to crimson the swaying walls.
   The hands cast shadows on the crimson walls.

   The candlelight shrinks and flaps wide.
   The shadows are full of old tenters—
   men curious as to the fashion of cities,
   men eager to taste newtasting bread,
   men wise to the north star and to the moon's phases,
   to whom East and West
   are cloaks pulled easily tight,

worn jaunty about the shoulders:
Herodotus, Thales, Democritus,
Heraclitus who watched rivers,
parian-browed tancheek travellers,
who sat late in wineshops to listen,
rose early to sniff the wind off harbors
and see the dawn kindle the desert places,
and went peering and tasting
through seas and wastes and cities,
held up to the level of their grey cool eyes
firm in untrembling fingers
the slippery souls of men and of gods.

The candle has guttered out in darkness and wind.
The tent holds firm against the buffeting wind,
pegged tight, weighted with stones.
My sleep is blown up with dreams
about to wrench loose and soar
above wormwood-carpeted canyons
and flinty sawtooth hills,
up into the driven night
and the howling clouds.

Perhaps when the light clangs
brass and scarlet cymbals in the east
with drone and jangle of great bells,
loping white across the flint-strewn hills,
will come the seeking tentless caravans
that Bilkis leads untired,
nodding in her robes
on a roaring dromedary.

2. Képis, two caps, a felt hat and a derby, headless on the rack; a muffler
dangles, an umbrella. My hat among them. The doors swing. . . .
   Table, two rows of green white jowls (*comme on s'ennuie*) munching razorscraped jaws face the catsup bottles, pickle-pots; collars

constrict the veins on flabby necks; knives and forks tinkle with little zigzag acetylene glints (*dans ce sale pays*). Eyes in sideglances (*comme on s'ennuie*) purse minds in tight (*dans ce sale pays*) like clasps on the mouths of pocketbooks.

My shoes creak as fed I make discreetly for the swinging door.

And yesterday
I rode a grey stallion
into the first olive garden
and day before yesterday
squatted in the full wind
I ate dates fried in ghee
at the right hand of Jassem er Rawwaf
in the red cave of firelight,
and watched Hassoon staunch the blood
from his cut foot in hot embers
and leaned my head back on the bale
of stringy yellow Persian tobacco
eyes gashed by the sharpscented smoke
legs pricked by the sharp desert flints,
and listened to Saleh
teach his frail thirsty song
of parched Hosein and Kerbela
to slenderwaisted Ali
whose walk when calling and calling
he led back to camp the fortytwo camels
was a procession of kings returning darkly
carved on a mountain
in triumph,
and wondered
watching the barbed flames of wormwood
why Nuwwaf rode off that day
on his great whitebearded dromedary
without eating bread

curlybearded Nuwwaf,
wind lover, cunning in the four directions,
who when he laughed brandished steel
out of kholblackened eyes.

Esch Scham

XII. HOMER OF THE TRANS-SIBERIAN

AT THE PARIS EXPOSITION OF 1900—but perhaps this is all a dream, perhaps I heard someone tell about it; no, it must have happened— somewhere between the Eiffel Tower and the Trocadero there was a long shed. In that shed was a brand-new train of the Trans-Siberian, engine, tender, baggage coach, sleeping-cars, restaurant-car. The shed was dark like a station. You walked up wooden steps into the huge dark varnished car. It was terrible. The train was going to start. As you followed the swish of dresses along the corridor the new smell gave you gooseflesh. The train smelled of fresh rubber, of just-bought toys, of something varnished and whirring and oily. The little beds were made up, there were mirrors, glittering washbasins, a bathtub. The engine whistled. No, don't be afraid; look out of the window. We were moving. No, outside a picture was moving, houses slipping by, bluish-greenish hills. The Urals. Somebody says names in my ear. Lake Baikal. Irkutsk. Siberia. Yangtse, Mongolia, pagodas, Pekin. Rivers twisting into the bluish-greenish hills and the close electric smell of something varnished and whirring and oily moving hugely, people in boats, junks, Yellow Sea, pagodas, Pekin.

And the elevator boy said the trains in the Metro never stopped; you jumped on and off while they were going, and they showed magic lantern slides and cinematograph pictures in the Grande Roue and at the top of the Eiffel Tower . . . but that must have been years later because I was afraid to go up.

I've often wondered about the others who had tickets taken for them on that immovable train of the Trans-Siberian in the first year of the century, whose childhood was full of *Twenty Thousand Leagues* and Jules Verne's *sportsmen* and *globetrottairs* (if only the ice holds on Lake Baikal) and Chinese Gordon stuttering his last words over the telegraph at Khartoum, and Carlotta come back mad from Mexico setting fire to a palace at Terveuren full of Congolese curiosities, fetishes of human hair, ithyphallic idols with shells for teeth and arms akimbo, specimens of crude rubber in jars; and those magnates in panama hats shunted slowly in private cars, reeking with mint and old Bourbon down new lines across the Rio Grande, shooting jackasses, prairie dogs and an occasional greaser from the rear platform, and the Twentieth Century and Harvey lunchrooms and Buffalo Bill and the Indians holding up the stage and ocean greyhounds racing to Bishop's Rock and pictures of the world's leading locomotives on cigarette cards. O Thos. Cook and Son, here's grist for your mill. Uniformed employees meet all the leading trains. Now that Peary and Amundsen have sealed the world at the top and the bottom and there's an American bar in Baghdad and the Grand Lama of Thibet listens in on Paul Whiteman ragging the Blue Danube and the caterpillar Citroëns chug up and down the dusty streets of Timbuctoo, there's no place for the Rover Boys but the Statler hotels and the Dollar Line (sleep every night in your own brass bed) round the world cruises.

That stationary Trans-Siberian where the panorama unrolled Asia every hour was the last vestige of the Homeric age of railroading. Now's the time for the hymns and the catalogues of the ships. The railsplitting and the hacking and hewing, the great odysseys are over. The legendary names that stirred our childhood with their shadow and rumble are only stations in small print on a timetable. And still. . . . Or is it just the myth humming in our drowsy backward-turned brains?

Does anything ever come of this constant dragging of a ruptured suitcase from dock to railway station and railway station to dock? All the sages say it's nonsense. In the countries of Islam they know you're mad.

In the countries of Islam they know you're mad, but they have a wistful respect for madness. Only today I was fed lunch, beef stewed in olives and sour oranges, couscous and cakes, seven glasses of tea and a pipe of kif, by the extremely ugly man with a cast in his eye and a face like a snapping turtle who hangs round the souks buying up fox skins, in the company of his friend the tailor, a merry and philosophic individual like a tailor in the *Arabian Nights,* all because I'd been to Baghdad, the burial place of our lord Sidi Abd el Kadr el Djilani (here you kiss your hand and murmur something about peace and God's blessing) and they feel that even a kaffir passing by the tomb may have brought away a faint whiff of the marabout's holiness. So a pilgrim has a certain importance in their eyes.

They may be right, but most likely this craze for transportation, steamboats, trains, motorbuses, mules, camels, is only a vicious and intricate form of kif, a bad habit contracted in infancy, fit only to delight a psychoanalyst cataloguing manias. Like all drugs, you have to constantly increase the dose. One soothing thought; while our bodies are tortured in what Blaise Cendrars calls the squirrelcage of the meridians, maybe our souls sit quiet in that immovable train, in the darkvarnished newsmelling Trans-Siberian watching the panorama of rivers and seas and mountains endlessly unroll.

Now's the time for the Homeric hymns of the railroads. Blaise Cendrars has written some of them already in salty French sonorous and direct as the rattle of the great express trains. Carl Sandburg has written one or two. I'm going to try to string along some inadequately translated fragments of *Prose du Transsiberien et de la Petite Jeanne de France.* It fits somehow in this hotel room with its varnished pine furniture and its blue slopjar and its faded dusteaten windowcurtains. Under the balcony are some trees I don't know the name of, the empty tracks of the narrow gauge, a road churned by motortrucks. It's raining. A toad is shrilling in the bushes. As the old earth-shaking engines are scrapped one by one, the mythmakers are at work. Eventually they will be all ranged like Homer's rambling gods in the rosy light of an orderly Olympus. Here's the hymn of the Trans-Siberian:

> *In those days I was still a youngster*
> *Only sixteen and already I couldn't remember my childhood*

I was sixteen thousand leagues away from my birthplace
I was in Moscow, in the city of a thousand and three belfries and
    seven railroadstations
And the seven railroadstations and the thousand and three
    belfries were not enough for me
For my youth was then so flaming and so mad
That my heart sometimes burned like the temple of Ephesus, and
    sometimes like the Red Square at Moscow
At sunset.
And my eyes lit up the ancient ways.
And I was already such a bad poet
That I never knew how to get to the last word.
....
I spent my childhood in the hanging gardens of Babylon
Played hookey in railwaystations in front of the trains that were
    going to leave
Now, all the trains have had to speed to keep up with me
Bale-Timbuctoo
I've played the races too at Auteuil and Longchamp
Paris-New York
Now, I've made all the trains run the whole length of my life
Madrid-Stockholm
And I've lost all my bets
And there's only Patagonia, Patagonia left for my enormous
    gloom, Patagonia and a trip in the South Seas.

I'm travelling
I've always been travelling
I'm travelling with little Jeanne of France
The train makes a perilous leap and lands on all its wheels
The train lands on its wheels
The train always lands on all its wheels.

"Say Blaise are we very far from Montmartre?"

We are far, Jeanne, seven days on the rails

We are far from Montmartre, from the Butte that raised you,
*   from the Sacred Heart you huddled against*
Paris has vanished and its enormous flare in the sky
There's nothing left but continual cinders
Falling rain
Swelling clouds
And Siberia spinning
The rise of heavy banks of snow
The crazy sleighbells shivering like a last lust in the blue air
The train throbbing to the heart of lead horizons
And your giggling grief . . .

"Say Blaise are we very far from Montmartre?"

The worries
Forget the worries
All the cracked stations katicornered to the right of way
The telegraph wires they hang by
The grimace of the poles that wave their arms and strangle them
The earth stretches elongated and snaps back like an accordion
*   tortured by a sadic hand*
In the rips in the sky insane locomotives
Take flight
In the gaps
Whirling wheels mouths voices
And the dogs of disaster howling at our heels . . .

And so he goes on piling up memories of torn hurtling metal, of trains of sixty locomotives at full steam disappearing in the direction of Port Arthur, of hospitals and who es and jewelry merchants, memories of the first great exploit of the Twentieth Century seen through sooty panes, beaten into his brain by the uneven rumble of the broad-gauge Trans-Siberian. Crows in the sky, bodies of men in heaps along the tracks, burning hospitals, an embroidery unforeseen in that stately panorama unfolding rivers and lakes and mountains in the greenish dusk of the shed at the Exposition Universelle.

Then there's *Le Panama ou Les Aventures de mes Septs Oncles,* seven runaway uncles, dedicated to the last Frenchman in Panama, the barkeep at Matachine, the deathplace of Chinamen, where the liveoaks have grown up among the abandoned locomotives, where every vestige of the de Lesseps attempt is rotten and rusted and overgrown with lianas except a huge anchor in the middle of the forest stamped with the arms of Louis XV.

It's about this time too that I read the history of the earthquake at
   Lisbon
But I think
The Panama panic is of a more universal importance
Because it turned my childhood topsyturvy.
I had a fine picturebook
And I was seeing for the first time
The whale
The big cloud
The walrus
The Sun
The great walrus
The bear the lion the chimpanzee the rattlesnake and the fly
The fly
The terrible fly
"Mother, the flies, the flies and the trunks of trees!"
"Go to sleep, child, go to sleep."
Ahasuerus is an idiot
....
It's the Panama panic that made me a poet!
Amazing
All those of my generation are like that
Youngsters
Victims of strange ricochets
We don't play any more with the furniture
We don't play any more with antiques
We're always and everywhere breaking crockery
We ship

Go whaling
Kill walrus
We're always afraid of the tsetse fly
Because we're not very fond of sleep. . . .

Fantastic uncles they are; one of them was a butcher in Galveston, lost in the cyclone of '95; another washed gold in the Klondike; another one turned Buddhist and was arrested trying to blow up the Britishers in Bombay; the fourth was the valet of a general in the Boer War; the fifth was a cordon bleu in palace hotels; number six disappeared in Patagonia with a lot of electromagnetic instruments of precision; no one ever knew what happened to the seventh uncle.

It was uncle number two who wrote verse modelled on de Musset and read in San Francisco the history of General Sutter, the man who conquered California for the United States and was ruined by the discovery of gold on his plantation. This uncle married the woman who made the best bread in a thousand square kilometers and was found one day with a rifle bullet through his head. Aunty disappeared. Aunty married again. Aunty is now the wife of a rich jam-manufacturer.

And Blaise Cendrars has since written the history of General Johann August Sutter, *L'Or,* a narrative that traces the swiftest leanest parabola of anything I've ever read, a narrative that cuts like a knife through the washy rubbish of most French writing of the present time, with its lemon-colored gloves and its rosewater and its holy water and its *policier-gentleman* cosmopolitan affectation. It's probably because he really is, what the Quai d'Orsay school pretend to be, an international vagabond, that Cendrars has managed to capture the grandiose rhythms of America of seventy-five years ago, the myths of which our generation is just beginning to create. (As if anyone ever *really was* anything; he's a good writer, leave it at that.) In *L'Or* he's packed the tragic and turbulent absurdity of '49 into a skyrocket. It's over so soon you have to read it again for fear you have missed something.

But the seven uncles. Here's some more of the hymn to transportation that runs through all his work, crystallizing the torture and delight of a train-mad, steamship-mad, plane-mad generation.

I'm thirsty
Damn it
Goddam it to hell
I want to read the Feuille d'Avis *of* Neufchâtel *or the* Pamplona
    Courrier,
In the middle of the Atlantic you're no more at home than in an
    editorial office
I go round and round inside the meridians like a squirrel in a
    squirrel cage
Wait there's a Russian looks like he might be worth talking to
Where to go
He doesn't know either where to deposit his baggage
At Leopoldville or at the Sedjerah near Nazareth, with Mr. Junod
    or at the house of my old friend Perl
In the Congo in Bessarabia on Samoa
I know all the timetables
All the trains and their connections
The time they arrive the time they leave
All the liners all the fares all the taxes
It's all the same to me
Live by grafting
I'm on my way back from America on board the Volturno, for
    thirtyfive francs from New York to Rotterdam

Blaise Cendrars seems to have rather specialised in America, in
the U. S. preferring the happier Southern and Western sections to the
Bible-worn hills of New England. Here's a poem about the Mississippi,
for which Old Kentucky must have supplied the profusion of alligators, that still is an honorable addition to that superb set of old prints
of sternwheel steamboats racing with a nigger on the safety valve.

At this place the stream is a wide lake
Rolling yellow muddy waters between marshy banks
Waterplants merging into acres of cotton
Here and there appear towns and villages carpeting the bottom
    of some little bay with their factories with their tall black

133

chimneys with their long wharves jutting out their long
wharves on piles jutting out very far into the water

Staggering heat
The bell on board rings for lunch
The passengers are rigged up in checked suits howling cravats
vests loud as the incendiary cocktails and the corrosive sauces
We begin to see alligators
Young ones alert and frisky
Big fellows drifting with greenish moss an their backs
Luxuriant vegetation announces the approach of the tropical zone
Bamboos giant palms tuliptrees laurel cedars
The river itself has doubled in width
It is sown with floating islands from which at the approach of the
boat waterbirds start up in flocks;
Steamers sailboats barges all kinds of craft and immense rafts of
logs
A yellow vapor rises from the toowarm water of the river
It's by hundreds now that the 'gators play round us
You can hear the dry snap of their jaws and can make out very
well their small fierce eyes
The passengers pass the time shooting at them with rifles
When a particularly good shot manages to kill or mortally wound
one of the beasts
Its fellows rush at it and tear it to pieces
Ferociously
With little cries rather like the wail of a newborn baby.

In *Kodak* there are poems about New York, Alaska, Florida, hunting wild turkey and duck in a country of birchtrees off in the direction of Winnipeg, a foggy night in Vancouver, a junk in a Pacific harbor unloading porcelain and swallowsnests, bambootips and ginger, the stars melting like sugar in the sky of some island passed to windward by Captain Cook, elephant-hunting in a jungle roaring with torrents of rain; and at the end a list of menus featuring iguana and green turtle, Red River salmon and shark's fins, sucklingpig with fried bananas, crayfish in pimento, breadfruit, fried oysters and guavas, dated *en voyage* 1887–1923. 1887 must be the date of his birth.

Dix Neuf Poèmes Elastiques, Paris. After all, Paris, whether we like it or out, has been so far a center of unrest, of the building up and the tearing down of this century. From Paris has spread in every direction a certain esperanto of the arts that has "modern" for its trademark. Blaise Cendrars is an itinerant Parisian well versed in this as in many other dialects. He is a kind of medicineman trying to evoke the things that are our cruel and avenging gods. Turbines, triple-expansion engines, dynamite, high tension coils. Navigation, speed, flight, annihilation. No medicine has been found strong enough to cope with them; in cubist Paris they have invented some fetishes and gris-gris that many are finding useful. Here's the confession of an enfant du siècle, itinerant Parisian.

> *So it is that every evening I cross Paris on foot*
> *From the Batignolles to the Latin Quarter as I would cross the*
> *   Andes*
> *Under the flare of new stars larger and more frightening*
> *The Southern Cross more prodigious every step one makes*
> *   towards it emerging from the old world.*
>
> *I am the man who has no past.—Only the stump of my arm*
> *   hurts,—*
> *I've rented a hotel room to be all alone with myself.*
> *I have a brand new wicker basket that's filling up with*
> *   manuscript.*
> *I have neither books nor pictures, not a scrap of æsthetic*
> *   bricabrac*
> *There's an old newspaper on the table.*
> *I work in a bare room behind a dusty mirror,*
> *My feet bare on the red tiling, playing with some balloons and a*
> *   little toy trumpet;*
> *I'm working on* THE END OF THE WORLD.

I started these notes on the little sunny balcony at Marrakesh with in front of me the tall cocoa-colored tower of the Koutoubia, banded with peacock color, surmounted by three gilded balls, each smaller than the other; and beyond, the snowy ranges of the high Atlas; I'm finishing it in Mogador in a shutin street of houses white as clabber where footsteps resound loud above the continual distant pound of the surf. It's the time of afternoon prayer and the voice of the muezzin flashes like brass from the sky announcing that there is no god but God and that Mahomet is the prophet of God; and I'm leaving at six in the morning and there's nothing ahead but wheels and nothing behind but wheels. O Thos. Cook and Son, who facilitate travel with long ribbons of tickets held between covers by an elastic, what spells did you cast over the children of this century? The mischief in those names: Baghdad Bahn, Cape to Cairo, Trans-Siberian, Compagnie des Wagons Lits et des Grands Expresses Européens, Grand Trunk, Christ of the Andes; Panama Canal, mechanical toy that Messrs. Roosevelt and Goethals managed to make work when everyone else had failed, a lot of trouble for the inhabitants of the two Americas you have damned up within your giant locks. The flags, the dollars and Cook's tours marching round the world till they meet themselves coming back. Here in Morocco you can see them hour by hour mining the minaret where the muezzin chants five times a day his superb defiance of the multiple universe.

If there weren't so many gods, tin gods, steel gods, gods of uranium and manganese, living gods—here's Mrs. Besant rigging a new Jesus in Bombay, carefully educated at Oxford for the rôle—red gods of famine and revolution, old gods laid up in libraries, plaster divinities colored to imitate coral at Miami, spouting oilgods at Tulsa, Okla., we too might be able to sit on our prayercarpets in the white unchangeable sunshine of Islam which means resignation. The sun of our generation has broken out in pimples, its shattered light flickers in streaks of uneasy color. Take the train, they're selling happiness in acre lots in Florida. So we must run across the continents always deafened by the grind of wheels, by the roar of airplane motors, wallow in all the seas with the smell of hot oil in our nostrils and the throb of the engines in our blood. Out of the Babel of city piled on city, continent on continent, the world squeezed small and pulled out long, bouncing like a new rubber ball, we get what? Certainly not peace. That is why in this age of giant machines and scuttle-headed men it is a good thing to have a little music. We need sons of Homer going about the world beating into some sort of human rhythm the shrieking hullabaloo, making us less afraid.

XIII. KIF

Gare St. Lazare. A man is sitting by the window of a restaurant eating alphabet soup. Outside through the twilight sifting pink sand over the grey-pilastered station, green omnibuses blunder, taxis hysterically honk, girls and young men with white twilight faces come up out of the Metro; there is a redfaced woman selling roses, a man with a square black beard unfolds *Paris-Soir*. From seaweed-garnished counters spread with seafood: oysters, scallops, seaurchins, mussels, clams, lobsters, snails, shrimps, prawns comes a surging tidal smell of the horizon. The man by the window of the restaurant eating alphabet soup against his will stirs the letters slowly with his spoon. Seven letters have come to the surface—GO SOUTH. Resolutely he eats them. Stirs with his spoon again; two letters left—G.O.

What was the story of the Irishman with the false teeth who was a spy for the British Intelligence who was eating alphabet soup in the little restaurant at the back of the mosque of Nouri Osmanieh in Stamboul? He was shot by a woman supposed to be a Russian and they said he had read his doom in the alphabet soup. Why are there always so many X's in alphabet soup?

Among the crowds going in and out of the station stalk long resounding words of twilight. The city of gleaming asphalt is flat and tiny, desert under the last scaring expansion of the summer day.

The other station is full of light, a refuge from the empty dusk. The train is packed with people and valises. In the nick of time I slip into the eighth seat in a third-class compartment. There is not room in the compartment for sixteen legs of assorted sexes, for sixteen perspiring arms. In the aisle you can stand up and smoke and see the suburbs of Paris, devastated and smouldering with dusk, at last decently buried by the advancing night. The train rakes up a picturebook landscape with inquisitive fingers of light as it rattles along wailing like a banshee. The trucks rumbling over the rails sing a jiggly song: Mort aux vaches aux vaches aux vaches. Mort aux VACHES.

The train is racing neck to neck with another train, gaining; windows, faces, eyes blur and merge into memories gulped by the hollow roaring night, fade into other trains; the Congressional gnawing into the feverish Maryland springtime, slamming the picket doors of shanty yards full of the funeral swaying of lilacs; the Black Diamond; the nameless train from nowhere into nowhere, the bobbing tassels of the blueshaded lamp, the looking out through eyes stingingly weighed down with sleep at the red yellow vanishing flowers with twisting petals, dark bottle-shaped bulks and unexplained word, blastfurnaces; the train folding itself up into the ferry to cross the bright mica of the Gut of Canso; the speeding express of the Trans-Siberian speeding to Pekin that never left its shed. Too many trains, too many wheels clattering over crossings, strange names spelled out in the night, goodbys at ticket windows, last meals gulped hastily at lunchcounters, hands clasped over suitcases; the head of the girl at the crossing you see on the body of a trackwalker down the line, hungry eyes looking through grimed panes, smiling lips shattered into void at the next station, questioning eyes of brownarmed gangs resting on their picks.

I have slipped back into my place between the highbusted lady in serge who sleeps with a handkerchief over her face and the starched Annamite who sits bolt upright. Opposite, a newly married couple strangled by their new clothes are stickily asleep; her head leans against a pillow in the corner, her mouth is open; his red winedrinker's face is burrowed into her shoulder. The windows are closed. You could dent the air with your finger.

Waking up with the sun in my eyes I sit watching the long blue shadows of black cypresses. At a spick-and-span creamcolored station the air smells of roses and garlic and dust: le Midi.

At Beni Ounif the air was sheer white fire. It was scaring to stumble off the beer-sticky diningcar into such hugeness. A black boy in a red fez carried my bag to Madame Mimosa's. On a bed in a shuttered room I stretched out. The train was leaving the station, hooted, puffed, rumbled away into the rocky desert. From very far away the lessening sound of wheels over rails, then silence. Silence becoming dense with sleep.

The sun had set. The sky had hardened into flaming zones, topaz, emerald, amethyst. Outside my door leaning against a pillar of the porch still warm from the sun, looking out into the vast desert square hemmed by low buildings with crumbling ochre-pink porches. In front of the crenelated station three toy freightcars. Nobody in sight, not even a dog. Size expands and contracts with the changing flare of the sky. Striding out of the tiny square, down the infinitesimal street, I trip over a purple mountain. I put out my hand to touch the white wall of a house; it is a mile away across the railroad tracks. The spiky cluster-headed grass is palmtrees striding in ranks through a gash in crimson rock. Beyond the houses the trodden stone falls away into an immeasurable canyon that turns out to be a sandy runnel made by irrigation water. Wondering whether I was still asleep I stumbled down a rocky path admiring the great river valley; I stepped in it. It was a little stream broad as my foot seeping through a crack in the mudwall of a dategarden. Meanwhile night was fast screwing down a glistening lid on a dimensionless chaos. A cool wind blew. Towards the town a few campfires were twinkling. A row of twitching mounds were camels asleep; there were muffled figures round the campfires. In doorways there were lamps, shadows about them. In a bare white room at a corner three Algerian soldiers were drinking against a green bar. They told me Madame Mimosa's was on the next corner. There walking through a small conglomerate store you came into an empty diningroom lit by a hanging lamp tightly shuttered to keep the light from trickling out into the night.

After a supper of turkey and desert truffles and white wine from Philippeville to stride out of doors again into the street without footsteps. The low flatroofed houses are obliterated under the stars. Silence is stretched taut across the night. I walk gigantic above the flattened houses, suddenly shrink with a drop like an express elevator from under the soaring stars, tiny manikin tottering on infinitesimal pins, to the tiny throbbing of a heart, frail squirts of blood through a tangle of infinitesimally tiny pipes. On the taut night comes a dribbling of watery notes from a reed, the softest drumming of two tired hands. The man who ate alphabet soup against his will is forgotten. The Irishman with false teeth is forgotten. The cool bright notes of the reed ripple out of everywhere; the drumbeat rising, deepening, is modelling breathless stately landscapes out of darkness. The eastbound southbound American who ate alphabet soup against his will takes refuge in his room, beside the wide creaky bed, in the protection of the smoky lamp, out of the path of these moving dunes of sound. This is the solitude and the voices crying in the wilderness. He gets undressed, cleans his teeth, sorts his clothes, works out a few lines of Lucretius, pretends he's in Buffalo, Savannah, Noisy le Sec, Canarsie. The trickle of the flute has parched away into the hurrying driven dunes of the drumbeat. St. Anthony alone in the wilderness of dark flesh, the intricately throbbing wilderness.

But the Irishman with the false teeth wasn't killed in Stamboul. He didn't dare go to a hospital, so the Russian woman and her husband took care of him in a shed in an old sheep corral in the outskirts of Top Hanep. They all three made jumpingjacks and the girl whose name was Olga sold them in the evening in front of the Tokatlian. She sold more than jumpingjacks, and all night the husband who had been an officer in the Russian navy without ever going to sea sat polishing his high boots and groaning. The Irishman groaned on account of the pain in his shoulder and for the loss of his false teeth. They talked in French the rest of the time, lying in abandoned army stretchers they used for beds. The Irishman, whose name was Jefferson Higgins, was a Gaelic pantheist. In a broken-down creamery in County Cork, he had had long talks with the Little People in his youth. The Russian officer believed in chastity, in macerating the flesh with alcohol to burn the devil out of it. In spite of that he never drank. Olga believed in hunger, fear, and the Virgin Mary. She hated men except those she loved. Through the long August days they lay in their stretchers talking of these things while the cicadas shrilled and kites wheeled in the cloudless sky. She loved them both and bought them food and washed their clothes and hung them to dry on the roof of the shed. She loved them both and petted them and called them her little grandchildren.

The naval officer blamed the misery of their days on what he called the helpless Russian soul; the Irishman blamed it on the British government; Olga blamed it on mankind. The two men, if it hadn't been for their lice and for the difficulty of shaving, would have been completely happy.

One morning Olga came home with a copy of the Communist Manifesto. It was in three languages, Russian, Armenian and Georgian. It had been given her by a taxi-driver from Odessa who had been an ornithologist. He had taken her to his room and set her up to a meal, but in the morning he had had no money to give her, so he had given her a copy of the Communist Manifesto.

They translated it for Higgins the next day. The husband and wife cried and kissed each other. They must have a faith, they told each other. From now on they would work for Russia, for the communist Christ, savior of mankind. They must work to go home. Olga would have to give up the Virgin Mary, she was too much like the czarina. They would work as carpenters and make furniture for the new Russia. He would stop making jumpingjacks; she would never prostitute her body again. If necessary they would starve. Immediately he started building a kind of settee out of a few old boards, to get his hand in; she watched him with bright eyes.

Meanwhile Jefferson Higgins walked up and down gnawing his ragged sandy moustache with toothless gums. The wound wasn't healing properly; he suspected he had syphilis. He wanted a new set of false teeth, cleanliness and fresh linen and Piccadilly and the military club. He was sick of the unceasing chatter of the two Russians; if he'd had a gun he would have shot them both dead.

When he had Olga alone he asked her with tears in his blue eyes to take him to a communist meeting. There must be communist agitators among all the Russians in Constant'. His life had entirely changed since that night when she had shot him in the shoulder. Thank God she hadn't killed him, she broke in, kissing him on the forehead. He would never work for the British again. He would go home and fight for Irish freedom. He would hand over all the secret codes of the Intelligence Department to the Bolos. The naval officer came home and found them in each other's arms. He wants to join the communist party, she explained. The Russian grabbed the Irishman and kissed him several times on the head.

Next day Jefferson Higgins with a cigar in his mouth and a panama hat on the back of his head sat in a small room in the Pera Palace typing a report with one hand. He was clean shaven, his moustache was neatly trimmed. He wore a neat grey flannel suit. His arm was strapped to his chest with clean bandages. He had a mouthful of teeth; they didn't fit very well but they were teeth. He was typing out the description of a Bolo plot to assassinate the High Commissioners, spread mutiny in the Allied armies and with the help of the discontented Turks seize Constantinople for the Soviet government. Occasionally he stopped typing and blew smoke rings. There was a soft triple knock on the door—Kitchener, said Jefferson Higgins in a low voice. A stout grizzled man in the uniform of a British colonel came in—It's not Kitchener today, it's Baden-Powell, growled the colonel— But I knew your voice. He picked up some typewritten sheets off the table and let the breath go out in a whistle between his teeth—It'll be a jolly fine bag I'll tell you. . . . We'll clean the blighters up. The High Commissioner'll feel pretty cheap when he sees this. You know where to leave it?—Yes, sir. Without another word the colonel laid on the table an American passport, handsomely outfitted with visas and made out for Fernald O'Rielly, travelling for a Chicago manufacturer of agricultural machinery, and a letter of credit on Lloyd's Bank— Report December 15th in Shanghai according to orders 26b, was the last thing the colonel said as he left the room.

Jefferson Higgins typed and typed. When he had finished the cigar he rang the bell for a whisky and soda. The waiter was a Bulgarian and read English perfectly. While he was making change he glanced at the typewritten sheets. Certain names on it were familiar to him. When he got down to the bar again he sent out a compatriot of his who was washing glasses in back to deliver a message to a bearded man sitting beside the mechanical piano in a small bar in a side street in Galata playing backgammon with a onearmed Greek sailor. As a result when the British military police went round at midnight to make the arrests certain of the more weighty birds had flown.

But Jefferson Higgins was already far down on the Sea of Marmora on the steamboat of the Lloyd Triestino. It was a moonlight night. He felt molten and tender as he used to feel as a boy when he thought of the Little People and the high kings of Ireland. His Gaelic was a ladle skimming rich thoughts off the milkwhite sky. The girl with the white arms working the butterchurn. The way a white shoulder sometimes peeped out from her dress. He began humming "Kathleen Mavourneen," shouted to the barman to bring him a gin fizz, went back to humming "Kathleen Mavourneen." Marseilles 'ld be the first place he could get a decent meal. The Bristol. He must find a nice sympathetic girl. Getting too old to care for the wild ones. For a week he'd live like a sultan. Then he'd settle down, look up Makropoulos and make some investments. About time he started thinking of the future, of his old age. He sat watching the great dry curves of the hills shining in the moonlight. The boat was going through the Dardanelles.

Meanwhile the British were combing Pera for Russians. Several men shot themselves. Olga's husband knocked out a sergeant with a blow in the stomach and was promptly shot through the head by a nervous recruit. The Russian refugees suspected of bolshevizing were herded into a basement. Most of them didn't care what happened to them; many were glad of the opportunity of getting a square meal. Then those considered most dangerous were weeded out and taken to detention camps. The rest were loaded on a scow and towed up into the Black Sea in the direction of Odessa. But Olga didn't go with them. In the company of a French interpreter she got out of Constantinople and eventually turned up in Algiers in the establishment of a certain Madame Renée, fifty francs to the girl and fifty to the house. Wherever she went she carried her zinc-white firmly modelled body carelessly as one might carry a chair across a room.

No one ever knew how Olga managed to get to New York—perhaps as somebody's wife. Anyway the dense clattering life all about her in the East Side tenement where she lived made her feel happy although she was tired all the time. Best of all she liked the Five and Ten Cent Stores and the blue trolley cars on Second Avenue. She sang nights in a little joint far east on Seventh Street. But she looked too much like a schoolgirl when she sang. The other girl, a dark Jewess who had been to Panama, got all the applause with

> *A thousand miles of hugs and kisses*
> *O ... poppa ... here we are*
> *O so far ... from Omaha.*

When we arrived in the open space among the crumbled houses of Findi the Caïd and his brother who had been a tirailleur came out to meet us. I presented my letter and black Mahomet made a little speech. We sat in the guest-chamber, a tiny whitewashed room with a running blue border of grapeleaves interspersed with the imprint of a hand at regular intervals. They brought out dates and sour milk. They were people of the Beni Amour, pure-blooded Arabs whom the French had planted in the oasis left desolate by the flight of the native Haratine and Berber people who had originally built the ksar and tended the dategardens. The wells were filling up and the sand was encroaching on the palms. When the guest dish had been eaten up we walked slowly and with dignity around to see the notable things of the oasis, the place where the battle had been between the Joyeux and the ksourians, the old wells, the dam built by people in the olden time, the vegetable gardens, the place where a foreign lady had pitched her tent and remained for five days, the tumbledown monument to the French soldiers killed in the battle, the wheel-tracks of the great autocar with six double wheels that had passed carrying officers in gold-braided hats to Timimoum. In the mountain that hemmed in the oasis to the south lived a demon named Dariuss, guarding a great treasure of gold. He rolled down rocks on people who tried to climb up there.

After dinner of ta'am with sweet milk poured on it and eggs we drank tea and sat long by the little light of two pigeon lamps talking. Eventually they forgot me and I leaned back against the wall, letting the great waves of Arabic eddy over my head. In pauses in the conversation you could hear no sound. The six or eight men who lived in the oasis were all in the room. Probably their wives were listening through chinks in the wall. Outside of the little patch of habitable houses were the broken houses of the old ksar, the tall datepalms and the immensity of sun-licked rock where only the demon Dariuss kept watch.

A great listless quiet was in men's faces, the energy of their words was mere ripples in quiet. In everything they sought the quiet that was the peace of Allah the merciful, the compassionate. It was what Achmed and his friend the tailor said in Marrakesh while Achmed was chopping the fresh hemp for the pipe of kif—In America we drink stimulants to make us excited, I had said—Here you smoke kif to make you feel peaceful. He couldn't make out what I meant. Excited was what he had been when the mule had run away and he had ran after it and lost his slippers, a miserable feeling worse than sickness. I tried to explain Coney Island, people paying money to be shaken up, jostled, ruffled, to slide down chutes, to roll in barrels, to jiggle on broken-back bridges. Achmed decided we must be mad in the western lands, but there must be a baraka in our madness because we were very rich. He handed a pipe to the little tailor, who took it reverently, smoked it between sips of tea and sat quiet looking out through the tall door at the sky, a drowsy smile at the corners of his mouth. Then Achmed inhaled deep and sat looking at nothing with a blue glaze over his eyes. He handed the pipe to me. The Westerner, the eater of alphabet soup, drew in the pungent smoke perfunctorily. Was there enough kif in the world to drown the breathless desires, the feeling of headline events round the next corner, the terrible eagerness of railroad stations at dusk, the twilight madness of cities, the wheels, the grinding cogs, the sheets of print endlessly unrolling? For Achmed none of these things existed. Life lay in quiet submission, life's fulfilment was life's brother death.

That night at Findi in the little guestroom of the Caïd's house, sitting back listening to the longdrawn quiet talk, I thought of those things, and of graven images and alphabet soup and the torture of the four directions and the squirrel-cage of the meridians, and of the train of the Trans-Siberian eternally about to leave, the engine whistling on the new train, shiny, smelling like new toys and rubberballs, that never left its shed at the Exposition Universelle. Who will find a name for our madness that has taken the place of glory and religion and knowledge and love, contagion subtler and more lasting and more full of consequences even than the pox Columbus brought back from the New World? Is it worth the drowsiness of kif and a man alone in the sheer desert shouting the triumphant affirmation: *There is no God but very God; Mahomet is the prophet of God?*

XIV. MAIL PLANE

IN THE LEE OF THE TIN SHED squat an old man and two women muffled to the eyes in tallow-colored rags. A mechanic kneading a piece of waste between his hands is kidding them about pork in a gentle drawl of French mixed with pidgin Arabic. Everybody shivers in the huge flow of cold east wind. At last the plane comes skimming the roll of the bare Moroccan hills. The women giggle behind their veils. In the name of God, says the old man and looks impassively at the passenger and the bags of mail and at the propeller blades that jerk round more slowly and more slowly, become two and stop. The passenger climbs in and huddles facing a thinfaced melancholy man with goggles; they drop in the mail, then the engine roars, the tin shed runs away, the hills waltz slowly, and white Tangier and the Straits and the Atlantic and the black cloud-dribbling mountains of the Riff spin gradually away, dropping in a lopsided spiral. The plane bounces like a ball across a snowy floor of white clouds. You're very cold and a little sick and the hours trundle by endlessly until all at once you are being sucked into a vortex of flying mist and sunny red plowed land and yellow and white houses, you circle the bull ring and it's Malaga. No time for lunch.

At Alicante the passenger sits drinking Fundador with the pilot in a kind of cabaret. On the stage stout ladies out of the past stamp tiredly to castagnettes, but at the table Mercedes (1926 model) slips into an empty chair. Her little black head is shingled, she makes goldy-round eyes like a cat at the talk of speed and cold airpockets.

In the hangover at dawn with hot eyes and dry tongues they start off again, grinding into the north wind.

Valencia through rifts in a snowstorm; then hours of bronze-green sea and rusty coasthills and a double corkscrew into Barcelona. No time for lunch.

North of the Pyrenees the air is thick like white soup. Over Cette the clouds are spouting in gigantic plumes. Trundle and swoop and sudden sideways skidding in the blinding whirl of a storm. It's terribly cold. The earth is dissolved in swirling mist. No more restaurants, steam-heated seats in trains, election parades, red fire, beefsteaks. Nothing but the speed of whirling cold over an imaginary sphere marked with continents, canals, roadribbons, real estate lots. An earth weird as Mars, dead cold as the moon, distant as Uranus, where speed snaps at last like a rubber band. Huddled in a knot, hard and cold, pitched like a baseball round the world. . . . Until you meet yourself coming back and are very sick into your old black hat.

CPSIA information can be obtained
at www.ICGtesting.com
Printed in the USA
LVHW05s0216110918
589689LV00006B/1105/P

9 781504 011488